your Faith on trial

Wallis C. Metts

 Bob Jones University Press, Inc.
Greenville, South Carolina 29614

Material from *Litigation in Education: In Defense of Freedom*, copyright 1977, by William B. Ball, is used with permission of the author.

Your Faith on Trial
by Wallis C. Metts
© 1979 Bob Jones University Press, Inc.
ISBN: 0-89084-112-8

To fellow pastors and educators
involved in the struggle for religious freedom
in the United States.

And to my daughters, Joy and Toy.

CONTENTS

PREFACE

Nothing in this book should be construed as legal advice, whether in the statements of the author, excerpts of statements by attorneys, or quotations from court transcripts and findings. The author writes as a clergyman and journalist, claiming no proficiency in the legal field. Whenever attorneys are quoted, it is possible to take their remarks out of context, since the full text of their remarks is not included. The same is true whenever the results of court cases are partially quoted. If pastors, educators, or other interested readers find themselves in situations similar to the ones examined here, they should seek competent Christian legal counsel.

This book was well underway before Bob Jones University agreed to publish it. The author has no past or present connection with the University. Although I agree with the stand taken by the University concerning religious freedom, I remain solely responsible for the findings and opinions stated in this book.

The reader should keep firmly before him the purpose of the investigative material included herein: to try to clarify for the Christian worker and layman the issues as they are illustrated by various litigations against Christian ministries, and to point out certain spiritual truths that become evident in the light of them.

Signal Mountain, Tennessee

ACKNOWLEDGMENT

Because of the large amount of quoted material in this book, it would be impossible in such a short space to list those to whom the author is indebted. I have tried to give credit in the text for all items for which I have the sources.

The inspiration for this book was furnished largely by the small army of pastors and educators across the United States who have taken a costly yet effective stand for what is right and true and Christian. Among these are the gentlemen of the Tennessee Association of Christian Schools.

I am grateful to the Rev. Levi Whisner, the Rev. Wayne Dillabaugh, Dr. Bob Settle, and the Rev. Rodney Peidot for furnishing me with excerpts of news stories and other items that shed light on the controversies in which they were involved. Special thanks is also due Brother Lester Roloff for sending me materials about his work.

The staff of the *CLA Defender* was especially helpful to

me in preparing this book. Their continuing coverage of legal battles facing churches across the United States is informative and trustworthy.

I am thankful to David Gibbs, chief counsel for the Christian Law Association, who took time out from his grueling schedule to review the manuscript for possible legal flaws.

Elmer Rumminger, Anita Ink, and others at Bob Jones University who worked patiently with me while I wedged this project in between numerous pastoral duties and Bible conferences have especially earned my appreciation. They have been very kind to me and have given me a new admiration for that venerable institution.

It was at Bob Jones University that Mrs. Roylin Hammond received the training that serves her well as one of my fine secretaries. She did much of the typing of this manuscript in her impeccable style.

My son, Wally Metts Jr., read much of the manuscript and furnished valuable insights.

One must not forget that trio of lovelies, my wife, Joan, and my two daughters, Toy and Joy. When their husband and father goes off world-conquering, occasionally coming home wounded and bleeding, they bind up the wounds with the understanding and compassion that only wives and daughters can give.

To all of these, and many more, thank you.

"We are principially and convictionally opposed to government control of the ministries of our church, and will do our best to apply that principle consistently and evenly in every area of our ministry as it becomes necessary."

—*Statement agreed upon by pastors in a meeting of the Tennessee Association of Christian Schools*

INTRODUCTION

Born again! It has become one of the catchwords of our times. With the nation's leading pollster, George Gallup, reporting a surging interest in evangelical Christianity, the Christian book market booming, and religious broadcasts now reaching as many as 20 million people at a time, many are hoping that God has begun to move upon the scene to turn the nation from the secular, materialistic path it has followed for nearly a century.

Such leading figures as Charles Colson and Eldridge Cleaver have shown dramatic evidence of religious conversion. It has even become politically expedient for the office-seeker to say he is "born again." The conservative religious bloc, estimated at forty percent, represents one of the strongest, most sought-after segments of opinion in America. A recent survey of leading high school students shows a dramatic shift toward the conservative viewpoint in the last five years.

The statistics are encouraging. Are we experiencing revival in America? The answer may depend upon how we react to another significant development in our national life that is testing the mettle of our faith.

It could be that God is permitting the pressure of government through its bureaucratic agencies to put our faith literally upon the witness stand to see if it is real! There are recent developments that are almost earthshaking in the bearing they have upon the faith of every Bible-believing Christian. It seems no longer possible for us to sit back and think it is a matter affecting only our Christian institutions. Properly understood, these new developments will force every Christian in America to face certain disturbing questions:

Do I really believe the Bible; is my faith real?

Do I have a heart conviction about Christ, or is Christianity merely a religious preference?

Am I willing to go to jail for what I believe?

Is my faith so strong that I would remain true to what I say I believe, even if my family were persecuted?

If I had to stand alone against the whole community, even other Christians, would I still stand?

How much of my life am I willing to change for my faith?

Believe it or not, every one of these questions has been challenged recently in American courts, and decisions have been rendered concerning them. And the future of your personal faith has been drastically affected. It is my hope to bring out the tremendous implications of these developments and what they have to do with you and your family.

Our government was begun on the proposition that God exists, and that He is above the state. The Constitution was scrutinized carefully by people in the churches of the infant country because it touched upon some very sensitive areas, such as what right the new government would have to control the church. As a result of that concern, the first ten amendments to the Constitution were ratified about twenty years later. The thrust of the First Amendment was to guarantee religious freedom. That guarantee was written into our national law because of the conviction that God is greater than the state and over the state, and not the other way around. That concept has now been seriously challenged.

This is of the most serious consequence to you, your children, your church, and your right to worship God as you please. It is now being said that the state is the people. Therefore, the church is subject to the state because it exists for the people. It is being said that since children are the people they belong to the state. The disturbing position has been taken in some quarters that the natural parent is only a temporary guardian of the child until or unless the ultimate guardian, the state, has occasion to remove the child from the supervision of the parent.

In addition, there has actually been a court decision defining precisely what kind of religious belief is protected by the First and Fourteenth Amendments. By implication, there are kinds of belief that are not protected. Do you have the kind of faith that is protected? What kind of faith is it? Is there any chance that you will ever be put on a witness stand to find whether you have that kind of faith? Or have you, in effect, already been put on the stand and tried for your faith?

It is my hope that we will find some readers who have the same quality of faith that Daniel and the three Hebrew children had—the kind that the Bible describes in the eleventh chapter of Hebrews.

1
YOU AND YOUR FAITH

Faith is a personal matter. One of the most cherished points of our doctrine is that the believer has direct access to God. Many of us, however, would be hard pressed to define faith or even to describe our own faith to others.

The biblical definitions are familiar to most of us. We know that faith means confidence. We know the Bible says, "Faith cometh by hearing, and hearing by the word of God." Almost all of us would say our faith is anchored to the Bible.

We know it has something to do with things one cannot see, since Hebrews 11:1 tells us that faith is "the evidence of things not seen." We have never seen God, yet we believe in Him. For most of our lives, that has not been much of a problem with us. We accept it as a standard dictum of our faith.

But now there is a problem with that. Certain developments in our national life have made it

necessary for people to demand that they *see* something to
assure them that we have the faith that we talk about. But
how can we reconcile this with what we have been taught
all our lives? If you can't see God and you can't see faith, how
can anyone demand that it be seen? How can you see
something that is invisible?

We cannot see atoms, but we know that they are there
because people have seen the evidence of them under an
electron microscope. Is there any way faith can be
examined under a microscope? In legal terminology, that is
exactly what some courts have done. Lawyers talk about
putting a person under "the microscope of cross-
examination." Through cross-examination they study a
person in the same way a scientist studies his subject
through investigation in a laboratory. The Christian faith,
as we know it, has actually been examined with that kind of
scrutiny.

Most of us are not used to having someone challenge our
faith in this way. We are accustomed to giving some pat
answer about how we feel about God. Some will say, "I
know it because I can feel it." Unfortunately, there has
never been a device invented that can record a feeling like
that, so it is not acceptable in court.

We may say, "I believe it because the Bible says so." But
what if somebody asked you, "Do you know, practice, and
live by everything in the Bible?" And suppose they said that
if you don't, it cannot be said to be a true basis for your
faith? What if they say you cannot claim *any* of it if you
cannot show by your life that you take *all* of it?

I may express my faith this way: "I believe in a God Who
is invisible, yet real, Who created all things and is over all. I
believe that He provides all my needs and I am supposed to
do what He says." But on a witness stand there has to be
evidence. They don't know if I am telling the truth. I may be
merely making a false claim. If I were on the witness stand
making a claim like that, and the prosecuting attorney
were trying to prove what I had was not a legitimate
religious belief, as protected by the Bill of Rights, how
could I prove my faith?

Suppose he said, "I can't just take your word for that. The law says you have to furnish some evidence." How could I go about proving that I really do believe in this God that he cannot see?

Is that a farfetched possibility? Not at all. It has been done recently, more than once. Christians have been forced by the courts to prove in just such a manner that their faith was real. And because such a precedent has been established it has an effect upon every other person who claims to share that belief.

It is one thing to say, "I have faith in God." It is simple to say, "I am born again." Anyone can say, "I accept Jesus as my personal Saviour," or "I am a Christian." But we realize that saying it is not enough. We all know that feelings are fickle and that people can be deceived.

It is during times when our faith is accepted and popular that it is easiest to be deceived about it. During those times it is simple to learn the language and go through the motions. That is why a current revival of interest in "born-again" Christianity may be dangerous for us.

During times of trial and persecution, on the other hand, there is a tendency to define the faith more sharply. Persecution has a tendency to separate the wheat from the chaff until only the real thing remains. Religious persecution, however, does not usually come in a frontal assault. History teaches us that it singles out a few adherents here and there and tests them for their faith. If it is seen that they are not any different from the rest of society, not offering any threat to the common lifestyle, they are considered harmless and left alone. If, on the other hand, they are considered a threat, a society that does not share that belief will begin to wage war on them in order to preserve the accepted way of life. For example, when a new king arose who considered the Hebrews a threat to the Egyptian way of life, he ordered all the males killed at birth (Exodus chapter one).

The history of ancient Rome provides another example. Probably no other civilization was so tolerant toward all religions as Rome. Although the Roman legions could force the people to do many things, they could not change their religious convictions. The Roman Empire for that reason took a tolerant view toward religious groups. The only thing required of them was that they be *licet*, or recognized by the state. The recognition was mutual. The state recognized a religion by written proclamation, and the religion agreed to the right of the state to approve its existence.

But the early Christians would not concede that Caesar had a right to approve the existence of God or their resurrected Lord. They refused to be declared *licet*. That's when the persecutions began on a small scale, and then became wholesale. The Roman government began to consider Christianity a threat to the state. Thousands of Christians died for their faith. The word *licet* is where we get our word "license." And licensing Christian ministries is precisely what the current trial of the Christian faith is all about.

The Romans devised a very simple test for determining if a person was a true Christian. The test was expressed in the cry, "Recant or die." If a person under threat of death would not deny he was a Christian, he was sentenced to die. If he changed his mind and decided that being a Christian was not that important to him after all, he was spared the death that the others suffered. After this became an accepted test, no Christian was ever safe. He was in danger of being hauled before the authorities at any time and having his faith tested in the same manner as others.

It would have been foolish to say, "Those cases only involve those other people. They have nothing to do with me." Every Christian knew that such was not the case. As soon as one Christian's faith had been tested by that criterion, it became possible to test every Christian's faith that way. The church was eventually forced underground because of the intense pressure upon Christians and their families.

The same thing is true in some countries today. All of us have heard stories, trickling out from behind the iron and bamboo curtains, of brave Christians who have stayed true

to their convictions in spite of persecution and death. We
have said, "There is no doubt that they really have faith in
Christ!" Their faith has been tested and found to be real. We
have thanked God that we live in a country where it is
usually not necessary to face such tests. But in a shrinking
world community, they do not stand alone! Even elsewhere,
every time a Christian's faith is tested in such a manner, it
reflects upon the life of every believer in America.

It is disturbing that those things did not start out as the
general practice. Before persecutions began on such a large
scale, precedents had to be set. A measure of consent had to
be obtained from the population at large, since even in a
totalitarian society it is impossible to govern a people who
refuse to be governed. It had to be done gradually and
discreetly through the ordinary channels of human affairs.

Let's imagine a typical conversation that might have
taken place between two believers when the restrictions
were only minor, and the persecution had barely begun.

"What do you think of this affair with Comrade
Bregzinski and the courts?"

"I don't know all the issues. I am praying for him, but
sometimes I feel he is just a troublemaker."

"I have noticed he talks about his case a lot, as if it is
requiring all his attention. Sometimes he even seems to act
like a martyr."

"Yes, I guess if the truth were known, he probably has
been careless in legal matters. If he had done a thorough job
and kept a clean house, the authorities would probably have
left him alone."

"I agree. Anyhow, I don't want to be too concerned about
political matters. I think the main thing is to get out the
gospel and build up other believers."

"I think you are right. It seems to me that just stirring up
the waters will bring discredit to the Christian cause. The
main thing to do is let these people fight their battles if they
want to, and not get others involved in them."

After eighteen years in the ministry, I found myself—a
Christian father, pastor, educator, and author—talking
exactly like that. But then as I began to get more

information on the matter, I became aware of some disturbing facts.

For one thing, I realized that I had no right to sit in judgment on these brothers who were going to court until I talked to them personally and got the information straight. To base my judgment about their trials upon faulty understanding is not only a poor way to make a decision, it is a sin!

In the second place, the more I learned about these people the more I came to understand that in most cases, they had never before in their lives shown any kind of troublemaking spirit. They were law-abiding citizens, going about their affairs with honor. It was not until some point of their faith had been challenged with legal and community pressure that they had suddenly been cast in the role of a malefactor.

But the worst was yet to come. The more I became exposed to what was happening, the more I felt myself comparing my own personal convictions with the issues that were being tried in these cases. And I could not escape the feeling that my convictions did not measure up. I found myself asking if my faith could stand the tests that were being applied in these cases.

I came to realize that in much of my Christian life I was applying the test: "Will this work? Is this the way to accomplish the task successfully?" But there was a gap between that question and the one being challenged on the witness stand. This question was not "Will it work?" It was "Is it right?" These people were risking reputation, money, and the very existence of their careers upon the question of whether or not what they believed was right. The thing that was being tested was the strength of their convictions—their faith! And the more I looked, the more I realized that when I really faced the issues in their true light, it was not their faith alone that was being tried, but mine as well.

It has been a painful experience, but I am thankful. I have tried to examine my faith under the microscope that the living Lord has permitted us to have focused upon our faith during this time. That microscope has been furnished through the courtesy of some men of faith who have experienced the pain of intense prying into their very hearts.

In the next chapter, we will take a look at some of the tests that have been laid down by the courts and how they relate to us.

2
WHAT IS A CONVICTION?

The Bill of Rights guarantees two things in reference to religious faith. It guarantees, first of all, that the United States can never establish an official religion. There is to be a clear difference between affairs of state and the practice of religion. We call this division of powers "separation of church and state."

The second thing the Bill of Rights guarantees is that there cannot be any laws passed that hinder the free exercise of religious faith. The First Amendment states that in all the laws necessary to the well-being of the state, there is to be nothing that would hinder a man from practicing his faith. After the Civil War, another amendment was passed that had a bearing upon religion. It takes the matter a little further by saying that even state governments could never pass a law restricting the free exercise of religion. The southern states resisted this amendment unanimously because it was felt that such a

law would put something on the books that must be tested.
As soon as it became the law of the land that states could
enact nothing to restrict religion, it was felt, tests would
then be necessary to determine what "nothing" was and
what constituted genuine religious faith. But the Fourteenth Amendment passed.

As government developed more services over the years,
it became necessary to regulate those services. In order to
protect the general welfare, the government formulated
standards and licensing procedures to cover any possibility
that public trust might be mishandled. Laws were passed
to cover these procedures. In order for them to be enforced
and regulated, numbers of people had to be hired to carry
out the law. These employees were not elected by the people
but hired by the respective government agencies. It often
became their duty to interpret the law and apply it to
specific cases. These nonelected government workers are
called bureaucrats. Their numbers have grown substantially in recent years.

In maintaining their respective jurisdictions, the
bureaucrats have discovered areas in which government
services overlap those carried on by religious groups.
Clashes between church and state have occurred, resulting
in court tests. Those in the religious sector have felt that,
under the terms of the First and Fourteenth Amendments,
the government representatives had no right to regulate a
religious institution. Bureaucrats have taken two positions:
one, that these religious institutions or persons had entered
areas that were not the proper concern of religion; two, that
in some cases the faith of the person or group was not of the
kind protected by the Fourteenth Amendment. In this
chapter we are going to see what has happened when the
latter position has been tested in the courts.

One of the matters vital to us is whether the state even
has the right to test this. The Constitution is a "delegated
powers document." That means that if the Constitution
does not spell out certain functions of government, then the
government has no power in these areas. Its powers have to
be specifically delegated by the people. Nobody has ever

found anything in the Constitution that gives government the right to try religious faith in the courts!

There is a growing concern that bureaucratic activity has entered many areas of private life never specified by the Constitution nor delegated by the people. And most of us continue to give consent to this by our silence. The position of the state has changed, in fact, so that it now considers itself all-powerful in areas not mentioned or specifically delegated. This effective reversal of philosophy by government agencies is seen by many as one of the most serious threats to our freedom since the founding of the thirteen colonies.

Conservative Christianity has usually aligned itself with forces that resisted this growing encroachment of power. Since Christians base their philosophy upon an unchanging Book, it is easy to identify with a document such as the Constitution which furnishes principles providing continuing guarantees for the citizens of the country. Because of this, Fundamentalists and other conservative Christians have often been pictured as religious rednecks who are just stubborn and don't understand the issues of a complicated, technological world. Usually, though, conservative Christians have had good, intelligent reasons to stand with the unchanging principles of their Christian heritage.

But the present crises go far deeper than conservative versus liberal political philosophies. The matter before us now is whether the church as we know it today even has a right to exist! Consider these developments:

Laws are now being considered in some states to license ministers. This licensing would govern not only the right to perform marriages and other activities but the very right to proclaim their message.

In some instances, criteria have been set up attempting to give the courts and their representatives the right to decide what activities a church is entitled to engage in. Some activities that have been questioned are day schools, daycare centers, youth programs, camps, Sunday schools, and even the Sunday morning service! It has been suggested, for instance, that a vacation Bible school is not a legitimate function of a church. This is only one area in which the state has taken the position that church functions should be tested in the courts. The Fourteenth Amendment is interpreted as giving the state grounds for testing the validity of a ministry to see if it is entitled to the protection promised by that document.

Those who have stood their ground in these cases have taken the same position taken by the early Christians in their confrontations with the Roman government: God is greater than the state; therefore the state has no right to interfere when God tells His people to do something. That presents a problem. The state does not deal directly with God. And representatives of government feel that they cannot take just anybody's word that he has received a message from God. But the courts do know that the Constitution of the United States protects a man's right to exercise his religious beliefs. How does one test whether a man's belief is a bona fide religious belief, or whether he is using it just to escape a responsibility required by the laws of the state or the regulations of a government agency?

David C. Gibbs Jr., an attorney from Cleveland, Ohio, has represented a number of clients whose beliefs were being tested. According to him, two things have been tested in the courts: first, what is a religious belief? and second, what is a church?

There are a number of things the courts have decided a church is not. It is not a building or a place. It is not an organization. Organizational structures change, but that does not mean the church changes. It is not a name. A church is not a church merely because it is called a church or assigned a religious or denominational name.

The courts have decided that a church consists of two things: beliefs and believers.

The question left to decide is whether the client is a believer, and whether he represents genuine religious belief. The courts have said that the Fourteenth Amendment does not protect all who claim to have religious persuasions. Believing that there are too many racketeers who could take advantage of religious protection, they feel that the claim for faith has to be substantiated.

According to Gibbs, two kinds of belief have been defined. One of these is called a *religious preference*. A religious preference is a strong belief. It may require faithful attendance at meetings. It could affect a person's behavior. It could be that he seeks to win others to accept his beliefs. A religious preference can prompt one to give generously toward a religious cause. But a religious preference is something that will change under certain conditions.

The second kind of belief is called a *religious conviction*. A religious conviction has all the characteristics of a religious preference with one exception: a person who has a religious conviction will not change his belief, even under intense pressure. And the state, through its courts, has been only too happy to provide the necessary pressure to see if the belief is really a conviction!

Gibbs says the state has found that there are certain pressures that will challenge the validity of a religious conviction. They include pressure on a man's family, community pressure, threat of prosecution, threat of imprisonment, and threat of death. Fortunately, the last of these has not yet been employed here in America. But all the others have been brought to bear upon believers in recent years to see if they will change their beliefs. If they change at any point, the court decides that they do not have a religious conviction, but merely a preference.

Although believing that the court has no warrant to sit in judgment upon our faith, we must concede that this provides a biblical test for faith.

This Christian lawyer has pointed to a striking biblical parallel for this in the case of the three Hebrew children (Daniel chapter three). After committing a breach of government commandment, they were given another chance to bow before the golden image. Their answer is a classic example of conviction: "O Nebuchadnezzar, we are not careful to answer thee in this matter. If it be so, our God whom we serve is able to deliver us from the burning fiery furnace, and he will deliver us out of thine hand, O king. But if not, be it known unto thee, O king, that we will not serve thy gods, nor worship the golden image which thou hast set up" (Daniel 3:16-18).

In other words, their actions were not based upon what was expedient, but what was right according to their faith. They were not going to change their belief even if God did not deliver them! Theirs was not merely a preference between the golden image and another god. Theirs was an unshakable conviction in the living God.

The following is a much condensed, paraphrased example of the kind of exchange that is taking place in these court cases. At issue is whether the person on the stand has a true conviction.

Attorney: "Mr. Smith, you say the activities in question were carried on because of your religious convictions?"

"Yes, sir, that is true."

Now the examiner is going to test that statement to see if the man on the stand is lying. Mr. Smith has been advised by his attorney to claim that his belief is a conviction. The lawyer for the state has been schooled in the way conservative Christians talk and think by experts who have studied "born-again" Christianity.

"Mr. Smith, do you have your beliefs written down in any form where they can be seen?"

"Yes, sir, I have."

"Where are they written, Mr. Smith?"

"They are written in the Bible, God's Word."

"Now, Mr. Smith, do you believe everything in this Book?"

"Yes, sir. Everything."

"Before we go any further, Mr. Smith, we are going to give you the opportunity to change anything in this Book you want to change. What is there you would like to change?"

"I'll take it just as it is."

The purpose of this line of questioning is to show that if the man on the stand does not live up to everything in the

Bible, he has in effect changed the basis of his belief! Because of the court's position that it is only by examining a person's lifestyle that his faith can be seen, the subject's lifestyle will be examined. Furthermore, if testimony can show that he has yielded under pressure and changed his beliefs, he has, in effect, shown his belief to be a preference rather than a conviction.

Now another trap is about to be laid.

"Mr. Smith, does this Book say anything about a person who would change this Book?"

"Yes, sir. It has something very definite to say about that. It says he is cursed."

"Now, Mr. Smith, since you say you have a conviction that this Book is the basis of what you believe and the way you should live your life, suppose you tell the court what this Book says."

Suppose Mr. Smith begins to relate what the Bible says and it is different from the copy the attorney is holding in his hand. At this point, many born-again Christians would fail. Many of them have not taken the time to study the Bible. For the most part, they have taken the word of a relative, a friend, or a preacher. And most of them who do have a clear idea of what they believe would not be able to take the Bible and find appropriate passages.

In examining a person's lifestyle to see if it measures up to his belief, the courts have said that they do not expect the person to be perfect, only consistent. An exchange similar to the following can take place.

"Mr. Smith, the law says you must send your children to a school approved by the state. You say that as a matter of religious conscience you must send your children to a private religious school that is not licensed by the state. You say it is a matter of conviction, is that right?"

"Yes, sir."

"Would you mind telling the court why your faith compels you to send your children to a school that is not approved by the state?"

"Well, sir, I don't like what the public schools are teaching the children. They are exposed to the wrong philosophy. They are taught that nothing is right or wrong, only relative. My faith says there are standards of right and wrong. Often, in the public schools, righteousness is debased and unrighteousness is exalted. I don't like the environment. Teachers and students dress immodestly and profanity and unwholesome language are heard in the halls and even in the classroom."

"And you say, Mr. Smith, those are the areas of your religious faith that have compelled you, as a matter of conviction, to ignore compulsory attendance laws and place your children in a private school?"

"I was simply saying that those are the reasons I send my children to a Christian school, sir."

"Tell me, Mr. Smith, do you own a television?"

"Yes, sir."

"Did you buy it?"

"Yes, sir."

"You invested, say, three to five hundred dollars in it, right?"

"About that."

"Mr. Smith, isn't it correct that your television will not turn itself on? In other words, you have to turn it on when you want to watch it, right?"

"Yes, sir."

"Mr. Smith, do you or your children ever hear any profanity or unwholesome language on television?"

"Yes, sir, I'm afraid so."

"Have you ever seen righteousness debased and unrighteousness exalted on television?"

"Well, yes, sir."

"Have you ever seen a woman on television who was dressed in an indecent manner?"

"Yes, sir, I'm afraid I have."

"I'm afraid I see a contradiction in your faith, Mr. Smith. You say you must break the law because you don't want your children exposed to these things. Yet you have invested a considerable amount of money in a device that not only exposes your children to the things you say you oppose on conviction, but does it consistently in the home in which you claim to practice your faith."

While television may be the most obvious area, it is not by any means the only area in which the courts have questioned the professed beliefs of Christians. And in some cases they have found practices that are very inconsistent with the Christians' profession.

What does the Bible say about the relationship between faith and practice? Is the court correct in assuming that if you have a religious conviction it will remain consistent in your lifestyle?

3

THE TESTING OF YOUR FAITH

Suppose you saw somebody call fire down from heaven or raise a corpse from the dead? Would that help your faith? Suppose staffs turned to snakes, water turned to blood, and the firstborn child died in every house in the land? Would that strengthen your faith? Such things happened to Israel, and still they got out into the wilderness and failed to believe God.

Even after they possessed the land promised them, God permitted a very strange thing to happen. He tested their faith in an unexpected way: "If there arise among you a prophet, or a dreamer of dreams, and giveth thee a sign or a wonder, And the sign or the wonder come to pass, whereof he spake unto thee, saying, Let us go after other gods, which thou hast not known, and let us serve them; Thou shalt not hearken unto the words of that prophet, or that dreamer of dreams: *for the Lord your God proveth you,* to know whether ye love the Lord your God with all your heart and with all your soul" (Deuteronomy 13:1-3; emphasis added).

God announced to the descendants of Abraham that He would actually permit false prophets to perform signs and wonders in order to test their faith! In these days of charismatic confusion, that is a sobering thought. God is testing our faith in many other ways today. And the Bible teaches that this process is necessary to prove, separate, and strengthen believers.

When Abraham, the prime Old Testament example of faith, was promised an heir who would be a blessing to the nations, twenty-five years elapsed before the birth of Isaac—years in which Abraham's faith was repeatedly tested. The testing of Abraham's faith was a *personal* matter, as well as an example to us. Even after the birth of Isaac, God tried the mettle of this patriarch's faith by asking him to offer his son as a sacrifice on Mount Moriah.

As a true believer, can you expect that God will bring tests upon you to reveal the genuine nature of your faith? Yes. The Bible speaks of "a great trial of affliction" (II Corinthians 8:2), "the trial of your faith" (I Peter 1:7), "others [who] had trial" (Hebrews 11:36), and "the fiery trial which is to try you" (I Peter 4:12).

Is it scriptural for our lifestyle to be examined in order to determine the genuineness of our faith? Yes, answers James. In his epistle, he affirms that we have no right to use the terms "born again," "faith in God," and other such phrases unless there is evidence of a corresponding lifestyle. "What doth it profit, my brethren, though a man *say* he hath faith, and have not works? can faith save him?" (James 2:14; emphasis added). Furthermore, James points out that this lifestyle must be one that is anchored to the plain commands of the Scriptures, rather than feelings, notions, or even outward success. "So speak ye, and so do, as they that shall be judged by the law of liberty" (James 2:12).

One of the things Fundamentalists are being tested for is their insistence that the Bible is the final rule of all faith *and practice.* It is not enough to say, "I believe the Bible." All issues, all behavior, all work are to be tried by the fundamental teachings of the Scriptures. It was when

Fundamentalists saw that their children were being subjected to an environment foreign to the practice of the Word of God that so many of them felt driven to the establishment of educational systems to provide that alternative lifestyle.

And now many of us are being put on the witness stand to see if our *practice* measures up to our *claim*. It is easy to drift. We have seen tremendous factors pulling the standards of the church downward. The media, the humanism in our schools, and the pressure of a profane society have had their effect upon us. Many of us have adopted behavior we had shunned a few years earlier. The world has watched our inconsistencies. Is God now permitting a legal assault on our faith in order to "separate the men from the boys" spiritually?

We have rejoiced in the banner of grace. We know salvation is a free gift, given eternally. We know that mere works cannot secure the favor of God, that He grants us His blessings only through the avenue of faith. But what kind of faith is it that ignores His commands? Someone has said, "Personalize the *commands* of God as well as His *promises.*" We love to fill in the promises of God with our own names. But faith also personalizes God's commands, realizing that they are as good for us as His promises. In fact, many of His promises are conditioned upon His commands. How inconsistent we are when we believe God, and yet refuse to believe the harsh results He warns of when we lay aside His commandments! James says that that kind of faith is not real at all. It is a dead faith. It is not the kind that saves.

It is relatively easy to say, "I believe in Jesus." But is that a *real* faith? One of the things early believers understood was that Jesus was not only Saviour, but Lord. "Saviour" speaks of His ability to save us from our sins, but "Lord" speaks of His absolute sovereignty over every area of our lives! Can a person believe in the Lord Jesus Christ without yielding to His authority as expressed in His Word? When it becomes popular, it is easy to say, "I'm born again." But the world has every right to expect the claimant to back up that statement with words and actions consistent with biblical commands.

When we get tough with ourselves and others in this way, we are often accused of being legalists. It is a popular notion that grace makes no demands at all. But we need to ask ourselves if the grace of God effects a change in our standing before God alone or if it is able to effect a change in behavior as well. Listen again to the Scriptures: "For the grace of God that bringeth salvation hath appeared to all men, Teaching us that, denying ungodliness and worldly lusts, we should live soberly, righteously, and godly, in this present world" (Titus 2:11, 12).

It is not only our bliss in a future world that grace brings. It also brings a change of life in this present world. Is it possible that Satan can use the Christian religion itself to beguile and confuse many? Has he made us believe that we can make some kind of mental assent to a creed without any corresponding inward change? Can he use flashy evangelists, beautiful cathedrals, and even signs and wonders to deceive people into thinking that they are Christians? It is possible. And it is also possible that a loving God, aware of the terrible danger of such a thing, would permit a certain amount of persecution and testing to throw real, scriptural faith into sharp relief. The reader might well ask himself if the kind of faith he has will stand.

The Scriptures indicate that not only individuals but *nations* are tested. One of the things history indicates is that because Israel was greatly blessed, she was also held more responsible. Is that true in America? We have built our society on freedom, particularly religious freedom. But now as a nation we are pleading the First Amendment more often for pornographers than for preachers. As a nation we seem to want freedom more for protestors than for protectors. We often want to protect the criminal more than the victim. Having given us great freedom, will God then not judge us more harshly if we greatly misuse that freedom? Is not growing government encroachment being used to test us as to whether we really *want* freedom? If God gives a nation religious freedom in order for them to worship Him, and as a nation they do not use it to worship

Him, is He under any obligation to let them use that freedom to rear their children in unbelief and degeneration?

Men are tested not only personally and nationally, but also *dispensationally*. In speaking of His personal return to this earth, Jesus asked, "Nevertheless when the Son of man cometh, shall he find faith on the earth?" (Luke 18:8). It is striking that Jesus asked this after telling the parable of the unjust judge.

I do not believe that the church will go through the great tribulation period which Jesus described in Matthew chapter twenty-four. But that is not to say that the church will not endure *any* tribulation. There are many believers facing unbelievable testing and persecution today. The purges in Russia and China probably caused the deaths of more Christians in a short period than any other persecution in history. Did God love those Christians any less than He loves American Christians? Do we have the idea that we are immune from the kind of suffering they endured? As the coming of Christ draws nearer, there may be a period of testing. As we examine the fast-moving issues of our day, we need to determine whether our faith is real.

4
WHAT IS A CHURCH?

The warm July air reminded me of how much I missed an air-conditioned car as I coaxed our ancient family jeep up the ramp of the parking garage across from Chattanooga's beautiful Blue Cross Building. My Florida vacation had been rudely interrupted by a call from our men to come back and meet with an attorney. As I walked into the lobby of the building, I asked the parking attendant if he knew where the meeting of the Tennessee Association of Christian Schools was being held.

"You mean that bunch of lawyers?" he asked.

"Well, it's mostly a bunch of preachers," I said.

"Anyway, there's only one meeting. It's on the tenth floor," he explained to me.

"These are strange times we live in," I remember thinking as I pushed the button that summoned one of the cylindrical elevators that carried passengers to the top of this glass-facaded building. I never thought I would be associating with lawyers so much as to be mistaken for one.

In the auditorium where this emergency session was being held, a group of clean-cut men moved about quietly. The mood was somber, yet assured. These men are used to having controversy swirling about their heads because they belong to the Christian school movement—a phenomenon that has shaken the educational establishment and brought consternation to government bureaus. By some estimates, there are more than 300 private Christian schools opening in the United States each year. They have become accustomed to dealing with fire marshals, welfare departments, and boards of education. But the business that brought me from Florida and other men from all over the state was a direct confrontation with the government of the United States.

I thought back to the first time our church had encountered resistance from the bureaucracy. When we began Berean Academy we wanted to offer the advantages of a Christian education to as large a segment as possible, so we decided to include a nursery school. It would give us the opportunity not only to begin teaching children at age two, but also to minister to working and single parents. When a letter came from the welfare department telling us we would have to be licensed, we wanted to do whatever was right. We began the licensing procedure, not knowing the dilemma we would find ourselves in.

As the requirements began to come to the attention of those who would be taking steps to meet them, our sharp administrator, John Innes, noticed something that disturbed him. There was a provision that the welfare department would have access to the files on parents and children. In addition to that, certain forms containing disturbing questions were to be filled out—questions like what the children ate for breakfast and how many other children they slept with.

"John, we just can't do that," I said when he called it to my attention. He agreed that it would violate one of our basic convictions—that the children were entrusted only to our care, and that we had no right to divulge this information to anybody.

A meeting was set up to explain to the lady handling the case why we could not meet this provision. We were told that it would have to be met if we were to be licensed by the state.

"Well, we want to do things right. But if we can get by without licensing, I guess we'll just have to do it," I replied. "Is there a law that we have to be licensed? What will happen if we do not obtain a license?" I asked.

"We will have to begin proceedings to close down your nursery school," she informed me.

That was a real shock to me. Here was a sweet lady sitting in our office threatening to shut down a ministry of Berean Baptist Church. It seemed incredible.

As it turned out, we were granted a temporary license for one year to give us time to conform. Meanwhile, legislation was introduced and passed that gave Christian school organizations in the state of Tennessee the right to police and accredit their own schools without interference by the state bureaus. We breathed a sigh of relief, not realizing that more difficulties lay down the road for us.

The lawyers in the Blue Cross Building were instructing us about what might lie ahead for us. We were in the process of filing a suit against the federal government and the state office of employment security. At issue is a ruling by Ray Marshall, Secretary of Labor of the United States. In 1976 Congress amended the unemployment tax laws, repealing the exclusion of coverage for employees of elementary and secondary schools, although churches were still exempt. Marshall, in interpreting the law, ruled that it also covers church-related schools. In a letter dated April 18, 1978, to The Most Reverend Thomas C. Kelly, General Secretary of the United States Catholic Conference, Marshall explained:

We believe that the repeal by Congress of the exclusion, in section 3309 (b) (3) of the Federal Unemployment Tax Act, of employees of elementary and secondary schools was clearly intended to result in State coverage of church-related schools, whose employees constitute over 80 percent of the employees of all nonprofit schools. In light of the repeal of 3309 (b) (3), we think the only services performed in the schools that may reasonably be considered within the scope of the exclusion permitted by 3309 (b) (1) are those strictly church duties performed by church employees pursuant to their religious responsibilities within the school.

The language in this opinion was of considerable concern to the members of the Tennessee Association of Christian Schools for a number of reasons. It was particularly disturbing that a government official could determine within such narrow limits what was and was not a legitimate ministry of churches. Such a ruling, if left unchallenged, could result in serious consequences for churches and unprecedented assault upon the separation of church and state. If the state can define what is the proper concern of churches, then any ministry of the church can become suspect. Under the supposed concern for the welfare of children, government agencies could then regulate Sunday schools, camps, bus ministries, and many other church ministries.

The ruling also was contrary to historical precedent. Public education in the United States is only about a hundred years old. Until that time, education was carried on by the church and other private agencies. The original institutions of higher learning in this country, schools such as Yale, Harvard, Dartmouth, and others, were all church schools. When a government agency takes the whole task of education, rules that it is only a secular concern outside the legal province of the church, and further rules that only a narrowly defined area of life is religious, it constitutes something new and ominous to Christian educators.

Our lawyers informed us that Catholic and Lutheran institutions were resisting the ruling on just such a basis. For years they had been lobbying for federal aid for their educational institutions and had been consistently told that their schools were church schools. By Ray Marshall's recent ruling, however, their schools had been redefined as secular and subject to taxation under the Unemployment Tax Act. Catholic and Lutheran officials were resisting the ruling in the courts on a policy basis, attempting to show that the government was being inconsistent in its policies.

To me and the people of Berean Baptist Church, however, the ruling was a serious affront to our religious convictions. We do not recognize life as being divided into two parts, sacred and secular. To us, all of life is sacred and is the proper concern of our faith. Our duties as parents are especially sacred. We believe that children belong to the Lord and that we are charged with the responsibility of rearing them for Him. We do not believe that we can abrogate that responsibility by dropping them off at an institution of learning.

It is especially disturbing to us that this very doctrine of secular and sacred divisions is taught and believed. The reason for establishing a school ministry in our church was to have the opportunity to teach reading, writing, history, mathematics, science, health, and all other fields of learning in their proper relationship to God and His revealed Word. We hold that unrelated facts in themselves do not constitute truth. In order for those facts to become truth, they must be properly related to reality as God has revealed it in His divine revelation. True facts can be taught in such a way as to arrive at a faulty and unchristian conclusion, giving children a totally unrealistic view of life.

Marshall's arbitrary ruling flies in the face of everything we believe. We were faced with the choice of either changing our convictions, ignoring them, or resisting this action by the government.

On May 9, 1977, the Tennessee legislature, acting on orders from the federal government, amended Tennessee Code Annotated 50-1309 to conform to the Federal Unemployment Tax Act. An interoffice correspondence from Sam McAllester Jr., Chief Counsel for the Tennessee Department of Employment Security, to Bob Waters, a department official, read as follows:

> If the church-related schools offer academic courses as their primary function and these courses are directed to and approved by the State Board of Education as a requirement for transfer from one school to another or for college

admission and such certification is issued by the State
Board, then it is our opinion that such schools would come
under the requirement for coverage of their employees
except those persons directly employed by the church. If the
non-profit school is primarily operated for secular purposes,
that is to provide a [sic] elementary or secondary education
to meet the requirements for admission to a high school or
college and the religious training received at such school is
incidental and not the primary object, their employees
would be covered for unemployment benefits.

According to Marshall's ruling, the providing of an
elementary or secondary education is a secular, not a
religious, concern. Although the interpretation of the
federal statute was not technically a law, state legislatures
were now changing their enforcement procedures to
conform with Marshall's opinion. The Tennessee
Department of Employment Security soon sent out forms
to all church schools in the state giving an option of whether
to become a taxpaying or reimbursement employer. When
we received our form and letter, not being aware at the
time of Marshall's ruling, we simply wrote them a note
informing them that we were a church school and not
subject to taxation. Many Tennessee pastors did the same
thing.

Wayne Webb, pastor of Macon Road Baptist Church in
Memphis, received a visit in June 1978 from a
representative of the department. When told that since he
operated a church and school he would be subject to
unemployment tax, Webb replied, "We don't have a church
and school. We only have a church. Our school is a ministry
of our church, just as the Sunday school or any other
ministry."

Armed with Marshall's decision and the amended
procedures of the state, however, the representative of the
state overruled Webb's appraisal of his own ministry. He
was informed that he was mistaken; that he did indeed have
two different kinds of endeavor, one sacred and one secular;
and that his school was subject to unemployment tax. He
was given until July 8 to comply or face assessment
proceedings. This would involve having his church's

records subpoenaed and legal action taken to collect the taxes retroactive to January 1978. Webb appealed to the Tennessee Association of Christian Schools for counsel and help.

Realizing the broad implications of this matter, Charles Walker, Executive Director of the TACS, issued a bulletin to all members of the association. In attorney David Gibbs's opinion, the issue violated three "immediate convictional beliefs":

1. *The definition of the church.* Our faith is structured as to what is the church and what is our faith and is handled by not what we think, but by what the Scripture dictates.

2. *The headship of the church.* Our faith dictates that Jesus Christ is the head of the church. We would be placing the government in a role over the church, thereby giving it a dual headship.

3. *Payment of taxes with church dollars.* The church schools are all underwritten to some degree by the tithes and offerings that come from the members of the church. To tax the church schools was therefore regarded as a taxation of the freewill offerings of the church.

The TACS asked for help from the Christian Law Association of Cleveland, Ohio, to fight the now very present danger. Since the majority of the churches making up the TACS are local church bodies not connected with any denominational body, it soon became evident that the fight could not be waged on an individual basis. The TACS decided to file a suit, giving the individual churches the option of voting about whether to participate. Attorneys and officers of the association had to move quickly because of the deadline given to the Macon Road Baptist Church; and I had flown back to Chattanooga from Fort Myers, Florida, to meet with attorneys, provide them with the information they needed to acquaint themselves with our ministry, and obtain a church decision on whether to join in the suit. We decided that we had no choice.

Our attorney wrote an article to inform us of the issues as far as our faith is concerned. After meetings with government officials, he explained to us the bureaucratic strategy:

"The attorneys in the Department of Labor have indicated to Christian representatives who have had conference with them on this matter that they are not sure that they could include church schools under this Statute (Law), but they knew that the churches would sue them and that the courts could then determine whether or not church schools were included under this Statute."

The opinion paper went on to explain that this action, if left unchallenged, would set a precedent that would leave the church schools vulnerable to taxation in all other areas, virtually putting them on the level of a private business.

The power to tax is generally considered a greater power than the power to regulate. Therefore, generally, if the Federal and State Governments can tax a church school, they probably can and will regulate that "church school" since it is not entitled to the Constitutional protection of freedom of religion because it is not a church or organization operated primarily for religious purposes. If the State can regulate a church school, then it can determine what courses may or may not be taught at a church school and who can or cannot teach at a church school. In short, if the position taken by the Secretary of Labor prevails this, in my opinion, "opens the door" or sets a precedent for the State and Federal Governments to, in essence, absorb private schools into the public schools or close private schools so that there are no schools other than "state schools." Since the state is prohibited from establishing a state religion, if this country only has state schools, then under our own Constitution, no "religious doctrine" can be taught in those state schools. Ultimately, the potential issue presented by this case is a battle over whether or not the church and the family have the right to educate their children regarding their faith (Christianity) or whether the State, alone, has the right to educate and train children.

Marshall's ruling raised the following biblical issues:

(1) Does the government or the Bible define what is a church?

(2) Who is the head of the church, Jesus Christ or the government?

(3) Does the government have the right to take the tithes and offerings of the church or do the tithes and offerings of the church belong to Jesus Christ?

(4) Do the family and the church have the right to educate their own children with respect to their faith (Christianity) or does the state have this right?

These issues have far-reaching implications for every Christian in America. Far from a fight confined to the state of Tennessee alone, this case will determine a number of questions. And all of us will have to ask ourselves if we are willing to let the government define what a church is. What is a church? What are the proper boundaries of its ministries? Who owns the children? Who runs the church? All of these questions will be tried in this court case. *And your faith will be on trial.*

On August 11, 1978, I received a letter from Dan W. Scates, Director of Unemployment Compensation for the Tennessee Department of Employment Security. In part, it read as follows:

> Complying with the U.S. Department of Labor requirements, we ... request that your organization complete and return within ten days from the date of this letter our form DES-210.1 N.P. with signature thereon .... If you fail to comply with this request, the department will assign a taxpaying account number.
>
> Reporting forms for first and second quarters of 1978 are also included for the reporting of your employees and their quarterly wages. Failure to comply within ten days, [will result in] assessment proceedings ... for taxes due.

It would have been difficult for me to believe it five years ago, but there it was. The church of which I am pastor was being taxed and threatened with assessment if the taxes were not reported and paid. I referred the matter to our attorney.

This leaves us in a difficult position in other areas of our ministry. For instance, we have voluntarily submitted to the regulations of the fire marshal's office. But fire marshals do not regulate churches to the degree they do schools. If we admit to their right to regulate us because we are involved in a school ministry, we are admitting that it is a different kind of ministry. When I recently mentioned this difficulty to an inspector, he replied, "No, you have a school. And schools are subject to regulation by the fire marshal."

We want our buildings to be safe, of course, and make every effort to make them so. But again, our schools are being singled out and given regulations that are different from those of other church ministries. As our case goes to court, we are reexamining our policies, our beliefs, and our convictions. What we say in court and the outcome of our case will establish precedents that will have a bearing on every church in America.

5
WHAT ARE THE REAL ISSUES?

Down the Intracoastal Waterway, forty miles south of Corpus Christi, Texas, a crew of boys maintains a fishing mission to provide fresh fish for the various ministries of the Roloff Evangelistic Association. The ministries, consisting of homes for alcoholics and wayward youth, and the Family Altar Broadcast, aired over 160 stations, are the special projects of Evangelist Lester Roloff and his helpers.

A wiry, indefatigable Texan, "Brother" Roloff, as he likes to be called, was born in Dawson, Texas, in 1914. At the age of nineteen, he took his milk cow to Baylor University to help pay his room and board, renting an old shed in an alley to have a place to keep his beast. After pastoring churches for twenty-six years, he entered the field of full-time evangelism. It was in those years of his ministry that he became burdened for the people in trouble he observed in churches across the country.

Since that time he has started two rescue missions and

eight homes. At the Help-Hers Home in Corpus Christi, next door to the Peoples Church, which Roloff now pastors, a sign above the front door reads, "All gentlemen must knock to be let in. Thank you." This home was begun when the older women being cared for, above the young adult age, were brought from the City of Refuge to the Rebekah Farm.

The Anchor Home for Boys is located at Zapata, Texas, ninety miles southwest of Corpus Christi. Many of the young men who live here are from jails and detention homes. A private Christian school is operated in this home, as well as in other Roloff homes. The Bethesda Home for Girls is located in Hattiesburg, Mississippi, and serves the needs of girls who are former drug addicts, runaways and unwed mothers. The City of Refuge is a home for alcoholics and other addicts located in an old antebellum home in Culloden, Georgia. In order to be admitted, men who come to this place must agree to stay ninety days. Another home, the Rebekah Home for Girls, is on 465 acres of farm land adjacent to the Peoples Church, just outside the city limits of Corpus Christi.

Brother Roloff's plan for restoring the unfortunate people who are sent to him is simple: take them away from harmful influences such as television, cigarettes, alcohol, and unwholesome companions, give them a good diet of fresh produce and fish, and feed them huge quantities of the Word of God. He has met with marked success. Even disinterested observers have admitted that he is doing a much better job than state institutions.

But it is the operation of these homes that has brought the evangelist into conflict with the state of Texas. In 1973 a licensed home near Houston, Artesia Hall, not connected with the Roloff ministries, burned down and suffered a fatality. The state began to crack down on homes. New codes were written requiring regulations and staff additions that were contrary to the convictions of Roloff's church and ministries. On August 3, 1973, the evangelist signed an injunction "under duress" to buy time for his homes.

The evangelist kept resisting any effort to have his homes licensed under the provisions of the State Welfare Office. In the November 1975 issue of his magazine, *The Liberty Bell*, he gave his reasons:

> I have never felt, and I know that I am right, that a church home needs a license from the Welfare Department any more than I need a license from them to preach or a license to operate my church. My convictions are built on the truth that Jesus Christ is the head of the church and that the Bible is the rule book, the Holy Spirit is the administrator and the keys have been given to the church and the gates of Hell are not supposed to prevail against it. God calls for an undershepherd to direct the affairs of His church and born again people constitute the body and are to be given to the manifold wisdom of God.

Brother Roloff was subsequently held in contempt of court when he refused to have his homes licensed or to shut them down. He was fined $5400 and released on $5000 bond. A later hearing before the Supreme Court of the State of Texas overturned the lower court's decision. Subsequent departmental rulings by the Welfare Department, however, negated the Supreme Court's decision, resulting in a court order to remove the sixteen- and seventeen-year-old occupants from the homes. They have been restored to the homes now, but Roloff has been in jail twice. The most recent appeal lost in the Supreme Court of Texas and the decision is being appealed to the Federal Court. In commenting on his struggles with the state of Texas, Roloff says, "A doctor friend of mine in Corpus Christi said the other day, 'Your case reminds me of a man who heard the desperate cry of a drowning child and jumped in the chilly waters and rescued that child. He was then prosecuted and sent to jail because of a "No Swimming" sign that was near the water where he saved the child's life.' That is about the truth. We heard the cry of drowning children nearly a fifth of a century ago and God knows, and you know, that we have been rescuing them."

The question arises as to why the state should fight the efforts of a successful clergyman who is doing a good job of caring for hundreds of troubled adults and young people.

Of course, many will say that Roloff is just a stubborn, old-fashioned preacher who ought to forget his stubbornness and yield to the progressive march of government standards. But the issue is not that simple. This preacher sincerely believes that his method of old-time religion is the very best remedy for the kind of people he ministers to. It is a religious conviction. And it is supported by the facts, since the evidence shows that the state homes, with all their standards and highly paid social workers at taxpayer expense, are not nearly as successful as his workers are. If the state standards cannot produce a better result, why then are they deemed superior? That is Roloff's stubborn argument, and it is devastating.

It is simple to think that because an organization has the state connected with it or approving it, it is superior. But the evidence does not support that assumption. Students in government schools, for instance, have consistently scored below students in private schools in standardized tests. The private schools are doing a better job, but the state is pressing to impose upon the private schools the standards and methods that are producing inferior results. The infinitely larger financial resources of government, the modern buildings, the assets of the large publishing houses, and the thousands of HEW regulations all have failed to produce the results being produced in often modest facilities with limited personnel. Private educators are insisting that it is because they maintain a controlled environment, avoid the frills, and hammer away at the basics.

Roloff has the same argument. He sticks to the basics. He gets results. The argument remains: can a bureaucrat, just because he is a bureaucrat, take better care of children than a preacher? Can a young, highly paid social worker do a better job than a seasoned minister of the gospel who has dealt with thousands of people and helped them solve their problems?

It is interesting that the findings showing more successful results are usually refuted or minimized. Preachers are not perfect. Some of them are even racketeers, although Brother Roloff has shown repeatedly that he is not. The opponents of these religious ministries, however, focus on anything they can find to accuse the ministers. They major on personalities to a large extent in many of the cases, hoping to discredit the ministries. Too often the press seems eager to report hearsay and gossip.

"Child abuse" is an ugly, emotion-stirring term. You can even get a hardened criminal in a prison stirred up with righteous indignation when you talk about abusing children. And the use of corporal punishment or harsh methods of discipline can bring community pressure upon the work in question. "We love children and want to protect them" is the message that comes across from the government agencies. In many cases that is true. Many dedicated case workers are sincerely interested in the welfare of children. A large number of the children sent to the Roloff homes are recommended by judges and case workers.

Many conservative religious observers, however, see a hollow and empty hypocrisy in the cry of "child abuse." In a case in Madison, Wisconsin, the Rev. Wayne Dillabaugh was accused of excessive whipping in his private school. The kindergarten child in question, Timothy Fischer, had bruises on his buttocks. The local press constantly took Dillabaugh to task over the incident. One citizen, however, asked in a letter to the *Madison Press Connection*:

> If child abuse was the only issue, and if the D.A. and the MPC [*Madison Press Connection*] were outraged at the bruises on "tiny" [D.A.'s word] Tim, allegedly put there by Dillabaugh, why was the same indignation so conspicuously absent during the trial in March, concerning the beating death of a four month old baby—the ultimate child abuse. The defendant in that case who admitted repeatedly striking the infant (who died from the resulting injuries) was charged by D.A. James Doyle, Jr. (that crusader against child abuse) with battery and failure to report a death. The sentence—six months in jail. MPC coverage of this case was most restrained indeed. Why? Wagner didn't even do a cartoon on it.

Why, indeed? Could it be because Dillabaugh is a

clergyman? Investigation has shown that an extremely
high number of the child abuse cases in the nation result
from the use of alcoholic beverages. Supporters of those
who use corporal punishment in homes and schools are
asking why there is no clamor to reduce the consumption of
alcohol. Observers point out that police officers cite the
marked contribution of pornographic literature, available
on newsstands everywhere for young children to see, to the
sex crimes they investigate. But the social workers and
members of the press are usually much kinder to sellers of
pornographic literature than they are to men they often
contemptuously call "reverends."

The case of Wayne Dillabaugh reveals the extent to
which a minister attempting to do a vigorous work in a
community can be exposed to hand-wringing, heated
criticism. One cartoon showed Dillabaugh dressed as a
comical shepherd, holding his staff dripping with the blood
of his victim, over young Timothy. Another showed
Timothy battered and broken, and with a black eye.

After the spanking incident came to the attention of the
press, Dillabaugh was severely criticized for his stand on
other issues as well. In the heat of the gay rights
controversy in Madison, one columnist lashed out bitterly
against him for seeking to uphold Wisconsin's laws against
unnatural sexual practices. This columnist called
Dillabaugh a gun-wielding, McCarthyistic pink-baiter
who was "gearing up for a war in which the obliteration of
civil rights for gay men and lesbians is only the first step."

The mayor of Madison, however, was not as concerned
with child abuse and gay rights as he was with something
else:

> Mayor Paul Slogin ... said the pastor is determined to
> "put the right people in office" and in an effort to get the
> supposedly "wrong" people out of office, he has announced
> that he will reveal the names of homosexuals who are
> currently involved in city and state politics.
>
> Slogin expressed fear that Dillabaugh would draw "a
> new wave of McCarthyism" into the city in next spring's
> elections.
>
> Mayoral aide James Rowen agreed and said that

Dillabaugh's campaign could shift Madison from "liberal-center to right-wing." He said that real issues like taxes and the environment may be "totally submerged to an emotional gut issue that terrifies some people."

Experts in human relations know that words like "child abuse," "civil rights," and "McCarthyism" are catchwords that stir the imagination and embroil personalities in conflict that is beside the main issues. Usually, however, in spite of Watergate, any utterance by a representative of government is treated with respect. Dillabaugh, condemned without trial by many of Madison's citizens and politicians, was acquitted by the court of any wrongdoing, but not before this victimized minister had lost half of his congregation and suffered enormous personal loss and indebtedness. I hardly know Dillabaugh, but it is a safe guess that he is at least as honest as the bureaucrats, reporters, and elected officials who battered his reputation and hurt his ministry.

In a letter to the editor, Dillabaugh's daughter expressed some of the hurt:

It makes me sick to read what people say they think about him, people he cared for and still does care for. The statement which upset me the most was the statement made by ——, a man Pastor Dillabaugh cared greatly for. This statement was "He [Pastor Dillabaugh] doesn't care about Madison or the people of Madison." That's a lie. I know because Pastor Dillabaugh is my dad .... If my dad didn't really care for the people of Madison he would have left here long ago. It isn't fun having people hate you and having your life threatened.

There are many honest questions we must ask ourselves. This is supposed to be a government "of the people, by the people, and for the people." But there is a growing concern even among law-abiding Christians that in some cases government bureaucracies have become a vested interest that feels threatened by concerned citizens and is abusing its power by striking back at the Christian community.

I do not think the issue is the personalities of Lester Roloff or Wayne Dillabaugh. I do not think it is child abuse or corruption. The issue is over who is going to have control.

Can a duly ordained and called minister control his own
ministry as God directs him, or must that control be yielded
to the state? The issue is religious freedom.

Both Lester Roloff and Wayne Dillabaugh claim that
they have the right, because of their religious convictions
and the constitutional guarantee of religious freedom, to
run their ministries as God dictates as long as they are not
destroying property or endangering the welfare of others.
The extent to which the state can challenge that right and
succeed is the issue that is being tried in the courts of the
land now.

That bureaucratic meddling touches even those who are
not members of the conservative religious community was
brought out recently by two syndicated columnists. Ralph
de Toledano reports in his column that confidential
government records are being sold to commercial
enterprises. In other words, the vast government computer
system, paid for by taxpayers, is being used against them.
De Toledano said:

> Medicare records contain the recipient's medical history,
> which even a doctor is not allowed to give out. They also
> include the subject's lifetime earnings, real estate holdings,
> drug and alcohol use, and marital status. All of this is
> supposed to be completely confidential and solely for the
> Social Security Administration's use.
>
> (Medicare knows more about your private life than any
> other government agency.)
>
> But now the General Accounting Office, a congressional
> watchdog agency, tells us that Social Security employees
> have been using those personal files for their own profit and
> selling them to many insurance companies.

One of the legitimate fears of churches and their leaders
is that growing meddling with the affairs of the church will
result in the collection of information which can eventually
be used against church members. But even the citizen who
is not connected with the church has reason to fear that
people in government are corruptible enough to use against
him information obtained by bureaucratic regulation.

In his column of August 19, 1978, William F. Buckley Jr.
brought out another danger: that government intrusion

into philanthropic concerns might dry up the voluntary giving and ministering to others by churches and other agencies. He said, "It quickly became a cliche, along toward the flowering of the New Deal, that the creeping institutionalization of charity might have the effect of contaminating the wellsprings of charity." Buckley mentioned an instance in Sweden in which an industrialist wanted to finance a public park. "There ensued not a testimonial dinner expressing the gratitude of the community, but a demonstration arguing that the park was a community facility .... Who does he think he is, to place himself in the role of the State, which is the only legitimate patron of the public?"

One of the problems of statism (the philosophy that the state is everyone's benefactor) is that public resources must be spread out to all the citizens to provide equal opportunity for all. That is, the state must control and operate benevolent facilities and programs in order to see to it that everybody gets his fair share. The fallacy of that kind of control is brought out in Mr. Buckley's column: "Fifty percent of the American people contribute only six percent of federal revenues. Accordingly, what you have is—on the assumption that the 50 percent paying the least taxes are a solid block favoring the contemplated Congressional philanthropy—a coalition of the non-taxpayers and some taxpayers, united in their resolution to exact from the balance of the taxpayers a contribution to the minimum income plan."

In other words, if a small minority is carrying most of the tax load, it is only natural for the "have-nots" who are in the majority to vote to take resources away from the "haves" who are in the minority and do not have as many votes. But in the arena of freedom, there is another subtle danger:

> But what will happen, down the road, in a democratic society when the acceptance of federal welfare programs relieves the individual of any sense of obligation to contribute to local charities? A Community Chest fundraiser remarks that this is—in his own experience—beginning to happen.
> How long will it be before we reach the stage, already

reached in Sweden and Great Britain, where the responsibility is assigned to the State? More important, what is the next likely development?

Many religious leaders fear the "next likely development" will be that the state will exercise so much pressure and entangle church ministries in so much bureaucratic red tape that many of the ministries the churches now perform will become impossible to perform, and that when the state takes upon itself more benevolent functions, freewill contributions and private funds for these works will vanish. But government cannot perform these as efficiently or as economically as the church can. Religious freedom is a matter not only of conscience but of sound economics as well.

6

WHERE DOES GOVERNMENT GET ITS POWER?

On the question of how Christian ministries fit in with government regulations, there must be a consideration of what the Bible says about government and its relationship to God and to the people of God. The Bible stories are full of the saints' involvement and conflict with the governments of this earth. Moses is placed in a little ark among the bulrushes in the river to escape the order of Pharaoh to wipe out the male children of Israel. The three Hebrew children face the seven-fold heat of the iron furnace for not bowing down to the golden idol. Daniel spends a night in the lions' den rather than bow to an earthly sovereign. Jeremiah defies the wrath of the king and languishes in a horrible pit. Joseph goes to prison for a crime of which he is not guilty. Mordecai stands against the vehement official, Haaman. Ezra and Nehemiah resist the local governments of the post-exilic period. The whole nation of Israel becomes subject to ungodly governments for more than four

centuries, and then again for seventy years. The apostles of
Jesus Christ are beaten, imprisoned, and commanded not
to preach in the name of Jesus, but they reply that they can
only follow the orders of their Lord. Paul writes his church
epistles from a Roman prison. John receives the Revelation
while in exile on Patmos. The Lord Jesus Himself is
condemned by a Jewish tribunal, tried before both Herod
and Pilate, and put to death as a common criminal.

Yet we are commanded to be good citizens and to
support the institution of government. Paul, the great
missionary apostle, writes to the saints in the very place
where he will one day become a prisoner: "Let every soul be
subject unto the higher powers. For there is no power but of
God: the powers that be are ordained of God. Whosoever
therefore resisteth the power, resisteth the ordinance of
God: and they that resist shall receive to themselves
damnation. For rulers are not a terror to good works, but to
the evil. Wilt thou then not be afraid of the power? do that
which is good, and thou shalt have praise of the same"
(Romans 13:1-3).

There can be no doubt that God does not encourage
anarchy or antinomianism (the philosophy that one is not
obligated to obey laws, rules, or moral standards). How,
then, are we to reconcile this plain command of the
Scriptures with circumstances in which believers must
choose between other commands of the Scripture and the
demands of an earthly government? Must we disobey
Romans 13:1-3 in order to obey other commands of God? Or
must we disobey other commands of God in order to keep
the commandment of Romans 13?

It is clear from Scripture that government is ordained of
God. After the flood, God gave Noah and his descendants
the authority to protect human life by instituting capital
punishment: "And surely your blood of your lives will I
require; at the hand of every beast will I require it, and at
the hand of man; at the hand of every man's brother will I
require the life of man. Whoso sheddeth man's blood, by
man shall his blood be shed: for in the image of God made he
man" (Genesis 9:5, 6).

It is a seeming contradiction to some who try to reconcile this with the sixth commandment, "Thou shalt not kill" (Exodus 20:13). But the Lord Jesus Christ gave the interpretation of this commandment: "Thou shalt do no murder" (Matthew 19:18).

A careful consideration of the Scriptures will show that the institution of human government is to enforce that commandment. To those who broke the commandment against murdering, there was a severe penalty. Their fellow men were given the legal authority to take the life of the murderer as a stern deterrent against violence and murder.

It is clear that the Scriptures teach us to be law-abiding citizens as a matter of conscience. It is impossible for a lawless person, rebellious in heart against legal and God-ordained authority, to maintain a clear conscience before God: "Wherefore ye must needs be subject, not only for wrath, but also for conscience sake" (Romans 13:5).

Further, the Bible makes it clear that believers are required to pay taxes and support the governments that serve them and protect them: "For this cause pay ye tribute also: for they are God's ministers, attending continually upon this very thing. Render therefore to all their dues: tribute to whom tribute is due; custom to whom custom; fear to whom fear; honour to whom honour" (Romans 13:6, 7).

The issue is quite clear. Those who have given their allegiance by faith to a heavenly King and Lord are also, as a matter of good conscience and proper testimony, to give their allegiance and support to earthly government. It is a principle repeated throughout the Scriptures and practiced by believers of every age. God does not put His stamp of approval upon a lawless, rebellious spirit.

In following this scriptural pattern, one must be aware of the whole picture of divine institutions. The family is one. But God makes it clear that His authoritarian structure for the family is not to be ignored simply because of the weakness of the family members. For instance, the children are still to obey parental authority even if the

parents are unreasonable or imperfect. The wife is still to
be in subjection even if her husband is an unbeliever and
disobedient to the Word, as long as he does not command
her to disobey Scripture (I Peter 3:1, Ephesians 5:22).

The church is another divine institution. Believers are to
seek a fellowship where the Bible is preached and Christ is
honored. Even though the leaders are not perfect,
Christians are to support and maintain that local
fellowship. The church as an institution is to be honored
and the local fellowship of believers is not to be ignored
(Hebrews 10:25). For a believer to absent himself from the
assembling of other believers because those believers
occasionally do wrong is to violate the plain command of the
Scriptures.

Government is a divine institution. For a believer to defy
government authority because its leaders are corrupt or
because government makes unreasonable demands upon
him is not in keeping with the plain commands of the
Scriptures. It is God's will for His people to be law-abiding
citizens.

Then why did Paul, the human author of Romans
chapter thirteen, write many of his epistles from a prison?
Why was he constantly in conflict with the state, frequently
accused as a lawbreaker and a traitor? Why did so many of
the great heroes of past eras of biblical history find
themselves in trouble with the law of the land? If these men
were true to God, faithful to His principles, and honored by
Him in His Word, why were they in conflict with earthly
authority? Is there a key to reconciling these seeming
contradictions?

The test is whether a command by government requires
one to disobey a clear commandment of God as revealed in
the infallible Scriptures. God has placed government over
us, but government must always be under God. He is the
higher authority. His laws are older and more enduring.
His truth is eternal. Systems of government come and go,
but God's Word remains forever. The Bible remains the
final authority for Christians. When an authority over us
conflicts with God's Word, then we, like the early disciples,

must obey God rather than man.

Some unscrupulous racketeers abuse this principle, excusing all kinds of violence and lawlessness in the name of religion. The Constitution protects a man's conscience and his religion from governmental interference; but, as we saw in chapter two, this protection applies only to religious beliefs that a man will not change, even under intense pressure. So we are talking about resisting the law not for personal benefit, but because our biblical convictions do not allow us any other choice.

There are certain situations, then, in which a Christian has the right and obligation to resist the law. One such situation is when there are *two contradicting rulings*. What is a law-abiding Christian to do when the ruling in question contradicts a law already established? In Ray Marshall's interpretation of the Unemployment Compensation Law, for instance, there seems to be a clear violation of two established laws. The first of these is the Constitution, which is the original law of the land. The First and Fourteenth Amendments prohibit a law that establishes a religion or prohibits the free exercise of a religion. In effect, Marshall has singled out an activity, education, and told the churches of the land that they cannot practice their religion in that field. That is a clear violation of the law as it is written in the Constitution. Many church leaders believe that his ruling is an *unlawful law*. In resorting to the courts to resist that law, then, pastors are convinced that they are the ones who are upholding constitutional law.

The second law that Marshall's ruling violates is in the area of taxation itself. There is a law on the books that churches will not be taxed. Marshall's ruling has the effect of taxing churches which operate schools. In the eyes of Christian educators working for churches, it is an unlawful tax. Which law does a Christian obey? Does he obey the established law of the land, or does he obey the contradictory ruling made by Ray Marshall?

A scriptural precedent is found in the book of Ezra. After seventy years of Jewish captivity in Babylon, Cyrus had decreed that a remnant of Jews return to Jerusalem and rebuild the Temple. Local authorities, however, were opposed to this effort by the representatives of the two tribes of Judah and Benjamin and appealed to King Artaxerxes, claiming the Jews were rebellious insurrectionists (Ezra 4:12-16). He commanded that the work be stopped (Ezra 4:17-24). This ruling was a contradiction to the law of Cyrus, given earlier. In the second year of the reign of Darius, the Jews appealed to him to search out the books of law in order to confirm that they were, indeed, operating under the edict of Cyrus. After determining that the law was on the books, Darius wrote a reply that is a classic statement of separation of church and state: "Now therefore, Tatnai, governor beyond the river, Shetharboznai, and your companions the Apharsachites, which are beyond the river, be ye far from thence: Let the work of this house of God alone; let the governor of the Jews and the elders of the Jews build this house of God in his place" (Ezra 6:6, 7). To paraphrase the king's commandment: "You fellows get out of there, don't bother the house of God, and let those people get their work done!" We know quite a few pastors around the country right now who would greet such an order with jubilation. Richard E. Riley, pastor of Emmanuel Baptist Church in Fort Myers, Florida, has pointed out that this ruling even prohibited the taxation of the house of God and its workers. Artaxerxes himself had commanded: "Also we certify you, that touching any of the priests and Levites, singers, porters, Nethinims, or ministers of this house of God, it shall not be lawful to impose toll, tribute, or custom, upon them" (Ezra 7:24).

Pastors and other church leaders who resist what they consider an unlawful attempt to tax the church have a clear precedent in the Scriptures and the law. It is interesting that these Jews in Ezra's day did not riot in the streets, declare war on the establishment, or foment violence. These Jewish leaders took the same route men of God are taking today—the legal right of appeal.

Another dilemma facing righteous people in their relationship to civil government occurs when there is *a law that requires its subjects to disobey a clear command of the Scriptures.* When the Jewish midwives in Moses' day were commanded to throw the male infants into the river, it was clear violation of the commandment of God not to commit murder. Shadrach, Meshach, and Abednego were commanded to bow down before an idol, a violation of the second commandment. Daniel was told to pray to an earthly king, a breach of the first commandment. The apostles were told not to preach the gospel, an order which, if obeyed, would have forced them to disobey the great commission given to them by their Lord. There are Christian patriots today who are absolutely convinced that the shortest road to ruin for America is to forget the commandments of God. As representatives of the Most High God, and as patriots and lovers of freedom, they are convinced that it is their duty to resist the efforts of men who would divorce our nation from the righteous commandments upon which its greatness was based and introduce an atheistic, humanistic society. Abraham Lincoln wrote in 1863:

We have been the recipients of the choicest bounties of Heaven. We have been preserved, these many years, in peace and prosperity. We have forgotten the gracious hand which preserved us in peace, and multiplied and enriched and strengthened us; and we have vainly imagined, in the deceitfulness of our hearts, that all these blessings were produced by some superior wisdom and virtue of our own. Intoxicated with unbroken success, we have become too self-sufficient to feel the necessity of redeeming and preserving grace, too proud to pray to the God that made us.

It behooves us, then, to humble ourselves before the offended Power, to confess our national sins, and to pray for clemency and forgiveness.

Romans 13:1-7 makes it clear that when God gave human authority in government, He never intended for it to be used against His people as long as they are doing what Scripture commands. Men in places of government have an obligation to realize that government is ordained and established by God. If government officials disobey the spirit of Romans 13:2, they also come under its warning:

"Whosoever therefore resisteth the power, resisteth the ordinance of God: and they that resist shall receive to themselves damnation."

When rulers are unlawful, they come under the condemnation of God as surely as anyone else. If America has a Christian heritage that is worth protecting, if she has religious freedom worth preserving, what then are we to do? Are the people of God merely to turn it over to the forces of atheism and humanism, or are they to fight to preserve religious freedom? That it is a contradiction of God's purposes in government for the state to persecute the church is clear: "For rulers are not a terror to good works, but to the evil. Wilt thou then not be afraid of the power? do that which is good, and thou shalt have praise of the same: For he is the minister of God to thee for good" (Romans 13:3, 4).

This is the situation God-fearing Americans find themselves facing. If Christians do not understand these issues and face them, who is going to do it? The so-called secular community cannot be expected to resist the march of secularism in our government and society. We will have to answer the question of whether we are willing to abandon our biblical convictions and national heritage to a secular, socialistic society that will rule over our children and grandchildren, or resist such forces, paying the price of fighting in the courts in order to preserve our heritage.

Attorney David Gibbs has pointed out that each time a Christian ministry or leader has to defend his convictions in court, it is not just that individual who has gone on trial. It is the faith and future of every believer in America. Indeed, it is America itself. In the following chapters we will meet more of the people who are involved in these important issues and learn what the issues are that are being tried.

7
TEMPEST IN A TEAPOT

On October 30, 1978, eight pastors, a few school principals, and the officers of the Tennessee Association of Christian Schools met with their attorney in a conference room of the Airport Hilton in Nashville. We came out of that meeting with the sobering realization that we might be involved in one of the biggest tests of religious freedom in the history of America. We were faced with the question of whether to "go for broke" on the question of government control over the church. If we followed through on the commitments that our convictions seemed to be forcing upon us, we might have to imperil our ministries and churches by resisting some areas of control over the church we had not seen as threats before. The next day, when forty pastors and other church personnel joined us, it became even more painfully clear. When we first challenged the right of the government to tax our ministries, we had bitten off a bigger chunk than we had realized.

Many things had transpired since Ray Marshall had given his interpretation of the revision to the Unemployment Tax Act on April 21. About one month later, on May 25, the Tennessee legislature had acted to enforce that opinion. Exactly fourteen days later, on June 8, Wayne Webb had been ordered to file status reports or face forced compliance. He was given a deadline of July 8, or one month. On July 7, one day before the deadline, Red Bank Independent Baptist Church in Chattanooga had joined the Macon Road Baptist Church of Memphis (pastored by Wayne Webb) as a codefendant and had entered suit in the Federal Court in Chattanooga. The Tennessee Association of Christian Schools and its attorneys had a sense of urgency in preparing its member schools in case the government also moved on them quickly. It was this urgency which had brought me back from Florida for the meeting at the Blue Cross Building in Chattanooga in mid-July. Then, on September 6, forty-one other churches, including Berean Baptist Church, had joined the original two churches in the suit.

On October 5, the first confrontation in the case occurred in Judge Frank Wilson's courtroom on the third floor of the Federal Building in Chattanooga. We had filed for a temporary injunction to keep the state from moving against us pending the main trial, which had been set for April 2, 1979. This hearing caught the court at an inopportune time, since Judge Wilson was hearing another history-making case. An independent group had been teaching Bible in the public schools in Chattanooga on a voluntary basis. The American Civil Liberties Union had joined a group of local defendants in bringing a suit to attempt to declare those classes unconstitutional. It was evident that, after hearing our case that day, he would have to wait a few weeks before rendering a decision. The federal government agreed not to hold the state agency in noncompliance pending Judge Wilson's decision.

Meanwhile, a number of other issues arose during the brief testimony of that hearing. The counsel for the U.S. had insisted, "These people want total immunity from all control by the government." I had researched enough of these cases to realize that he had, indeed, put his finger on the issue. The issue in every case against a church ministry had been, "Who is going to control these ministries?" In a meeting following the hearing, I suggested to attorney David Gibbs that I thought this was the main issue, and I was becoming painfully aware of some persistent questions that had to be answered in other areas. We had many other things to discuss concerning the question at hand, however, and we did not pursue the idea.

Ray Marshall, however, was persisting in his self-assumed role of defining a church's ministries. In an interview with AP correspondent Bob Harris, he made some revealing statements. According to Harris, Marshall said, "A church becomes more than just a church when it gets into secular things, and therefore needs to be regulated just like any other organization."

In his article, Harris quoted Philip Mason, public information officer with the Employment and Training Association, as admitting that this new regulation "might mean the beginning of the end of separation of church and state." Mason said:

> We've had separation of church and state up to now, but now the churches are being controlled just like they were part of the local government, and I guess they don't like this.
> But ... this really does not violate separation of church and state, because if the church is going to get into secular activity, such as serving food and teaching algebra, science and English, then it has to conform to government regulations. It has to, for instance, conform to public health laws, fire codes, building safety codes, and so forth. This unemployment tax is just another law it has to conform to.

Some of us were asking ourselves, "How many more areas and how many more laws?" Now even serving food had been defined as a secular activity! How much more of our lives would be deemed "secular" by government agencies until the church was under total control of the state?

Alluding to Mason again, Bob Harris had written, "He indicated a church can remain exempt from these laws as

long as it does what a church is supposed to do—preach the
Gospel and teach the Bible—but when it begins to do the
secular world's job, watch out."

We had objected to governmental definition of the
church's ministries on the biblical grounds that Jesus
Christ is the head of the church. Now, Marshall and Mason,
not even members of our church, were defining the limits of
our church ministries. As to our objections, Harris
reported, "He [Mason] cited the introduction of social
security and income taxes as payroll deductions back in
1934. He said he remembers how people complained that
the 'deducts' amounted to more than their net paychecks,
but in time they eventually accepted it as a necessary part
of life. So will be the case with the churches and the
unemployment insurance tax, Mason predicts."

They were betting on the hope that we would eventually
roll over, play dead, and forget the whole thing, accepting it
as a fact of life. The nagging questions remained: "How
many more things? How many more areas will we be
willing to accept as 'normal'?" And how many violations of
our faith had we already accepted as "normal"?

The October 30 meeting dragged on for hours. We knew
we were having to face some agonizing choices. Could we,
in principle, reject some areas of control on the ground of
the headship of Jesus Christ and accept others? Most of us
had taken for granted that some regulations were
necessary. At least we assumed they were. But how do you
define which ones are acceptable, and on what scriptural
grounds? We are standing on the Scriptures. Does the Bible
give the government the warrant to control the church?
Does the Bible ever assign education to the state? Does the
Bible, in fact, enjoin the church to teach history, math,
science, and home economics? If so, what are the passages
that do so? How about other religions, different from our
own? Are all of them entitled to First Amendment
protection according to our convictional beliefs? How can
we justify other things we had been accepting, similar to
unemployment tax, and now say we are opposed to the tax?

In the brief filed with the court, we had said:

It is this assertion of authority over plaintiff churches by the government which contravenes the foundational principle of plaintiff churches that the Lord Jesus Christ is the head of the church and the sole authority over it that the plaintiff churches object to and will never yield to. If plaintiff churches yield to the government as their authority over their churches, then the Word of God, the Bible, indicates that plaintiff churches are in peril of destruction and have engaged in grievous sin against the Lord Jesus Christ . . . .

Plaintiff churches see the consequences of the principle of the government's assertion of authority over their ministries which constitute the church and deny the principle in the same way that our forefathers did in the American War of Independence.

This same principle is a Biblical principle set forth in the Book of Daniel and in Acts where plaintiff churches are commanded to obey God rather than men when the government commands plaintiff churches to reject their faith or cease their faith. Therefore, plaintiff churches ultimately will "go underground" as in the Soviet Union or even die rather than reject the Headship and sole authority of the Lord Jesus Christ over plaintiff churches.

When the more than forty pastors from local, autonomous assemblies, without any prior coaching, came out of their meetings the next day without any dissenting voices, we had every reason to tremble. Perhaps, in His providence, God was moving among us to bring into the national limelight some important issues regarding our faith. And we had put ourselves in a position in which we were risking immediate confrontation. It was not going to be easy.

8
ENFORCING THE SECULAR SOCIETY

When Constantine was emperor of Rome (306-337), he professed Christianity and granted religious freedom to all Roman subjects, intending to end persecution of Christians. Theodosius (378-398) made Christianity the official state religion and made church membership compulsory. There had been major imperial persecutions in A.D. 96, A.D. 98-117, and continuing intermittently until A.D. 311. Under these persecutions the Christians had responded with a conquering faith and their numbers had multiplied.

But when Christianity became the official religion, the attitude of believers began to change. Instead of relying upon spiritual power and thinking upon spiritual realities, many professing Christians began to look upon their religion as the product and beneficiary of an earthly kingdom. The Christian religion took on a "secular" character. The word "secular" means "belonging to an age." The eternal began to give way to the temporal. Where once Christians recognized the priestly character of every believer, now they appointed themselves priests to carry out the "religious" functions, while the majority of the professing Christians went about their "secular" tasks. State-enforced membership filled the churches with unbelievers. Later, when the barbarians overthrew the Roman government and infiltrated their society, they also adopted their religion, bringing their pagan practices with them. Thus the Roman Catholic Church was born, and thus it has continued until this day.

Outside of this "official" church, a minority of believers still clung to the distinctives of the Christian faith as taught in the Bible. In every age they have resisted the "official" church, and have paid for their resistance with intense persecution. With the coming of the Reformation, these nonconformists grew into a much greater number, but many of the Protestant groups retained some of the characteristics of the papal Church of Rome. One of the ideas that remained among some was that life for Christians was divided into two parts, the secular and the sacred. Where the original believers looked upon life as totally God-oriented, some of their modern brothers saw some things as outside the proper concern of "religion."

This idea provided the background for a great deception. The idea of a "secular" society was eventually brought into sharp focus by the philosophy of Karl Marx. Marx concluded that all of life, as demonstrated by the march of history, was the result of a class struggle. Life was not a struggle between evil and good, between the holy and the profane. According to Marx, it was class against class, and the classes were marked off by material goods. The world is material; the meaning of life is best understood in considering the distribution of material goods. The greatest good is for the greatest number to have their share of the world's goods. Thus, the name of his philosophy of conflict: *dialectical materialism.*

The reason the communistic philosophy of Marx has been propagated worldwide with such religious fervor is that it is, in fact, a religion. Any system of interpretation about the world around us, reality, and man's past and destiny is a religion. That is why evolution, an important part of Marx's dogma, is a belief, a religion. The thing about Marx's philosophy that deceives so many is that it claims *not* to be a religion. It is, it says, a "secular" idea.

Most of the world has fallen for it. The politicians want their share of the goods. The unions want their share. The blacks want their share. The "women's libbers" want their share. When the voters of America go to the polls, they often vote for the politicians who will give them their share. Principle is cast aside. It is not "what's right?" but "what's in it for me?" that decides the way most Americans cast their votes.

This attitude feeds Marx's doctrine of *statism*, which teaches that the state is everyone's benefactor. He held that once men looked to some kind of supernatural god for their provision, but now that idea has been overtaken by the inevitable march of the socialist reality. According to Marx, the state is the only agent which can bring the greatest possible sharing of goods to the greatest number of people.

Much of our government philosophy has been affected by that idea. Our idea of government was originally one that limited the government to the power delegated to it by the people. But now, the state has assumed the role of provider. This idea has so pervaded our thinking that few seriously question anymore that the government owes each of us his share of social security, protection, and opportunity. Once government sees itself as provider, it considers itself responsible to enter every area of our lives. We have sacrificed our freedom upon the altar of our greed.

It is important for us to recognize that this is a *religious* idea. Man makes a god out of whatever he looks to as his provider. We may not admit it. We may even go on paying lip service to the God we once worshiped. But in reality, we are not looking to Him to provide for us. We are looking to the state. According to the Bible, where we look for our provision is where we place our faith. And if we are to

continue our faith in God we have a divine imperative: "But
without faith it is impossible to please him: for he that
cometh to God *must* believe that *he is*, and that *he is a*
rewarder of them that diligently seek him" (Hebrews 11:6;
emphasis added). In other words, faith is the understanding that God is the provider. *Providence*, a kindred word,
means that God is able to supernaturally arrange circumstances in order to care for us.

Statism explains many things in our world today. It
explains, for instance, the fanatical drive for "women's
rights." If the state is the benefactor, then it is the duty of
the state to guarantee sexual equality. President Carter
appointed forty-two people to the IWY (International
Women's Year) Commission set up by the U.N. Some of
their goals are twenty-four-hour day-care centers, paid for
and controlled by the federal government, for all children;
federally   funded   retaining   centers   for   "displaced
homemakers"; and mandatory school programs in sex
education and family planning, with contraceptives and
abortion information available to all students.

Among those appointed by Carter to this commission
were Bella Abzug (who was later dismissed), Gloria
Steinem, Jean O'Leary, and Eleanor Smeal, all leading
women's liberation proponents. Some quotations from Ms.
Steinem are revealing: "Overthrowing capitalism is too
small for us. We must overthrow the whole ——
patriarchy!" ("Patriarchy" is the word the women's
movement uses for the traditional biblical concept of the
family.) She further stated, "For the sake of those who wish
to live in equal partnership, we have to abolish and reform
the institution of marriage . . . . By the year 2000 we will, I
hope, raise our children to believe in human potential, not
God." Surely this indicates that Ms. Steinem has adopted
the religion of Karl Marx.

Statism is the pervasive philosophy behind the conflict
between public and private education. In the October 1978
issue of the *Tennessee Educator*, there appeared an article
entitled "The Tax Revolt, Strangler of Education."
Apparently the public educators feel they can't do their job

without their "fair share" of public resources. A month earlier, Billy Stair, in a *Tennessee Teacher* article on the conflict between the two sectors of education, described the exodus of "tens of thousands of students from the public school." He went on to make this significant statement: "Although the abrupt departure of thousands of Protestant children from the public schools posed a number of immediate problems, the most serious long-range impact for these school systems was a distinct loss of public esteem. [They are] left suddenly without the traditional political and financial support of the middle class."

There is no thought here that the state has failed in a task given to it by the people. The state is seen as the legitimate provider of education, and it has been "deserted" by the middle class, not the other way around. It does not occur to a devotee of statism that there are any other alternatives than to look to the state for all one's needs. But a recent study by CBS concludes that, although the cost of public education is now four times higher than it was in 1963, most parents feel that the state has failed in its role of providing an education. As Brian Richardson noted in the *Tallahassee Democrat*, "Seventy-six percent of the people surveyed favored back-to-basics education.

"Eighty-three percent opposed social promotion.

"Forty-one percent said their children are not getting as good an education as they did. Only 35 percent think their children's education is better.

"Eighty-four percent said discipline in the schools is not strict enough."

There is an overwhelming feeling that the educational system has deserted the people. One of the Christian's main objections to public education is the philosophy of *secular humanism* that prevails in the system. This philosophy ties in closely with Marx's teaching, focusing on man instead of God, on the present instead of the eternal, on the pursuit of pleasure instead of self-control, on the authority of "the group" instead of the authority of God's Word. It, too, may call itself "secular," but it is in fact a religion. The secular humanist's goal is to create a perfect society where

everyone is happy and shares equally in goods and
opportunity. This can be accomplished, he thinks, by
reliance only on man's ingenuity and resources.

Yet now that Christian schools have stepped in to correct
both the philosophy and the methods, there is a growing
movement to impose the unworkable and inferior
government standards upon the private schools, which are
doing a better job. Why? A revealing observation was made
by R. J. Rushdoony, president of Chalcedon, a research
foundation that provides materials to the Christian
education movement, in a letter to Daniel Carr, a pastor
who led in the struggle for Christian school freedom in
North Carolina:

> What we are facing is a war to the death between
> Christianity and humanism. The humanists know this, but
> all too many churchmen either do not know it or refuse to
> know it. In the USSR, there is a constitutional guarantee of
> freedom of religion. However, it is totally subject to permits,
> licensure, regulations, and control; as a result it is non-
> existent, except for the KGB-controlled churches which are
> maintained for public relation purposes. Although it is
> nowhere openly stated, it is clear that this same goal is in
> mind in the United States and throughout the world. Step
> by step, the hope is to bring the churches, Christian schools,
> missionary agencies, Christian foundations and other like
> institutions of our Lord into the hands of the state by a
> variety of small and large regulations . . . .
>
> The humanists are ungodly men, but they are not fools.
> They know that if the Christian schools continue to grow as
> they now do, by the end of this century we shall see a
> Christian republic emerging and humanism perishing.
> Hence, the intensity of their feelings and their warfare.

This California expert agrees that it is a religious
struggle between two viewpoints—Christianity and
secular humanism—that are so sharply opposed that they
cannot exist in the same system.

Part of the religion of secular humanism is the doctrine
of *behaviorism*—the idea that men are totally controlled by
their environment. They have no soul or moral compulsion,
nor do they have any supernatural reality over them. To
control the destiny of man, then, the state merely controls
his environment. This type of control is most effective

among school-age children, and for many years the behavioral psychologists have deeply influenced educational philosophy. Education is seen, not as an agency to help children gather facts, but as an agency to effect behavior changes.

U.S. Senator Orrin G. Hatch has noted this alarming trend and is attempting to forestall it. The Hatch Amendment, attached to the Elementary and Secondary Education Act of 1978, insures that "no student shall be required, as part of any applicable program, to submit to psychiatric examination, testing, or treatment, or psychological examination, testing, or treatment, without the proper consent of the parents."

Columnist James Kilpatrick, writing about the Hatch Amendment, says:

> The senator was determined to crack down on the arrogant curiosity of a gaggle of crackpot psychologists who have invaded the public schools . . . .
>
> In his remarks to the Senate last week, Hatch cited as a typical example a sex education program in Wisconsin that starts at the kindergarten level. In this "preevaluative training," children as young as ten are told how to get an abortion. He could have cited a hundred other programs that involve invasions of privacy. One questionnaire from California asks of . . . little girls: "Do you often see your father with no clothes on?"
>
> Sen. Hayakawa, in his remarks to the Senate, inquired rhetorically how such attitudinal tests ever got to be a part of public education. It is the result of a flourishing heresy, he said, a heresy that rejects the idea of education as the acquisition of knowledge and skills. Instead, the heresy regards the fundamental task of education as therapy.

It can hardly be missed that behavior modification and "messing around with the psyches of young people" are functions of a religion in which man is a god and human behavior is the ultimate reality. What has it cost us? One has only to look around. A new government survey concluded that now children run greater risks in school than on the streets. Although only twenty-five percent of students' time was spent in schools, it was reported that "40% of the robberies and 36% of the assaults on urban teenagers occurred in school." The report went on to say, "More than 5,000 secondary school teachers are attacked in an average month, almost 1,000 of whom require a doctor's attention for their injuries."

One disturbing thing is that, as part of their plan to use education to preach their religion, the social planners are thinking about copying the Soviet educational system. According to the Associated Press:

> With one of the most massive and highly organized child-care programs in the world, the Soviet Union has freed millions of mothers for work and provided their children—from 2 months to 7 years of age—with a place to stay from 7 a.m. to 7 p.m., or even overnight.
>
> The Soviet program, initiated in the 1920's, is one model that is being studied by the U.S. educators faced with a changing American society in which more mothers are taking jobs and looking for child care.
>
> "The U.S.S.R. is the first country with a mass centrally controlled pre-school program available to all and *designed to affect personality* [emphasis added]. We've been interested in it for a long time," says Janice Gibson, a University of Pittsburgh professor who has spent a half dozen summers here studying kindergartens . . . .
>
> The pre-schoolers are encouraged to cooperate with communal games and toys and to shun children who do not conform—a small-scale structure that mirrors aspects of adult Soviet society.

Marx is having his day in the field of education. But most Americans do not realize that their educational systems, paid for by their tax dollars, are carrying on programs designed to preach the Marxist doctrine of a materialistic world in which man is god. And too many of us are wrapped up in the same philosophy: "What can the state do for *me?*" It will take a wholesale renunciation of that idea before we can turn the thing around. Somehow, there must be a revival of the old-fashioned idea of voting for what is right, rather than voting for what is apparently profitable. The Bible puts the emphasis upon doing what is *right*, upon putting principle and decency above expediency. It is not really our government officials who have foisted this deplorable situation upon us. They are merely a reflection of our philosophy. And when the judgment of God falls upon us for having a false religion, it will not fall only upon Washington or upon our statehouses; it will fall on us and on our children. God says: "For I the Lord thy God am a jealous God, visiting the iniquity of the fathers upon the children unto the third and fourth generation of them that hate me" (Exodus 20:5).

We may already be seeing God's hand of judgment in our immoral and lawless society. There is now one abortion for every 2.8 live births. One out of two of our young people getting married now sues for divorce. Venereal disease is vaulting to frightening proportions. Drugs are rampant. Violence and vandalism in the public schools now cost as much as textbooks. Latest government statistics show that suicides among Americans ages fifteen through twenty-four more than doubled in a decade. In ten years, crime is up sixty-five percent for eighteen-year-olds and older and ninety-eight percent for seventeen-year-olds and younger. We have made the state our god and man our idol, and it has all come to a head in the dying, corrupt educational system we have built for ourselves. And yet, when some see the alarming trends and attempt to circumvent the cancerous philosophy of the humanists by building an educational system that is truly Christian in philosophy, the cry arises that the church is getting into something that is a "secular" function.

There can be no doubt that there are determined people who are dedicated to enforcing a secular society through the school system. And this sordid business is being carried out by the passing of laws and the enforcing of regulations designed to make it difficult, especially for those in the public schools, to resist the pressure of ungodly philosophies.

In Chattanooga recently, a high school coach was prosecuted for being too familiar physically with female students. According to J. B. Collins, Urban Affairs Editor for the *Chattanooga News-Free Press:*

> The attorney for the teacher, who denied all charges, claimed that his client had been placed in a difficult

situation in the school by having him teach physical
education to sexually mixed students [sic].

The basis for the charges against the male coach might
not have come about in the first place, the lawyer indicated,
if the school had had a man physical education teacher for
boys and a woman teacher for girls, like it used to be ....

The school principal had testified that it is true that girls
in the physical education and gym classes are "more
vulnerable" to situations that prompted the hearing
"because they dress down for the classes."

Supt. James Henry agreed that "it would be better" to
have men teachers for boys and women teachers for girls in
gym classes ....

But he insisted that "it can't be done" under federal
guidelines prohibiting segregation of students or teachers
on the basis of sex .... If the city schools are going to
continue to get federal money, the schools will have to abide
by federal rules, the superintendent said.

If we were dedicated to doing what is right, we would
tell the federal government to give their money to
somebody else. We would put principle ahead of money.
But we don't. It is the "system"; we feel helpless in it. And
there are people in places of power who know that. As long
as we are motivated more by material values than spiritual
values, we are their hopeless victims.

There are enough conscientious educators in the public
education system alone who, if they were motivated by
principle, would rise up and throw off the shackles of the
humanistic system. According to Paul Harvey in a
syndicated column on February 5, 1978, public educators
often send their children to Christian schools:

I don't know if you know, but Dr. Ernest Boyer—our
nation's Commissioner of Education—sent his own son to a
private school. Before Dr. Boyer became our nation's No. 1
public school official he sent his son to Loudonville, N.Y.
Christian School.

And that's not all.

Among all the parents who send their children to
Christian schools, the largest single professional group is
from public education. What this says is, that public school
teachers and principals—more than anybody—don't want
their own children in public schools.

Mr. Harvey goes on to describe some of the reasons:

In the beginnings of our nation, all our schools were church schools. Public education is a comparatively recent innovation.

The National Center for Educational Statistics reports the cost to taxpayers for educating a public school student grades 1-12 is $21,000. Tuition for 12 years for Christian school education averages $9,838. And the latter figure includes $1,200 for registration fees and books. So the cost of a private (Christian) education is now less than half the cost of a public school education. There is no longer any challenge to the claim that Christian schools are academically superior to public schools. Achievement test scores show that Christian school students are academically superior to public schools ....

Eighth graders in Christian schools are reading at 10th grade level. First graders, in all subject areas, are achieving at the 88th percentile. The national norm is 50.

It is not hard to see why many leading educators are trying to do away with the standardized tests. They show that the humanist experiment in education is a massive failure. It is much more difficult to see why these inferior methods and standards are being forced by law upon private Christian educators whose methods are producing superior results. But this blindness is in evidence everywhere one turns for information, and the only explanation is that it is a spiritual blindness.

The spiritual battle rages everywhere in the world today. It may take different forms in different societies and economic systems. But it is the same lie, and as long as we regard it as merely a political problem or an economic problem, we will continue to be deceived. It must be faced squarely for what it is: an attempt by gigantic spiritual forces to send our world crashing down around us. Many of the nation's Bible-believing leaders feel that all we can hope for is to turn back upon the mercy of the Lord and take some steps to correct our own behavior. Many are saying that we must pray for revival. That is true. But prayer is only one of the steps in the formula for revival (II Chronicles 7:14). God told the nation of Israel that there was something that was blocking their prayers: "Behold, the Lord's hand is not shortened, that it cannot save; neither his ear heavy, that it cannot hear: But your iniquities have separated between you and your God, and your sins have hid his face from you, that he will not hear" (Isaiah 59:1, 2).

It is very convenient for us to lay our troubles on our politicians or our educators or our ideological enemies around the world. But confessing their sins will not bring revival. It is only by recognizing *our own failures* and correcting them, no matter what the cost, that God will hear our prayers.

In his address at Harvard University in June 1978, Alexander Solzhenitsyn said:

> On the way from the Renaissance to our day, we have enriched our experience, but we have lost the concept of a Supreme Complete Entity which used to restrain our passions .... We have placed too much hope in political and social reforms, only to find that we were being deprived of our most precious possession: our spiritual life. In the East, it is destroyed by the dealings and machinations of the ruling party. In the West, commercial interests tend to suffocate it. This is the real crisis. The split in the world is less terrible than the similarity of the disease plaguing its main areas.

Solzhenitsyn said that the East and West are more alike than most of us think. It is a stinging indictment from a man who spent years in a Soviet labor camp. The only *real* difference, he says, is a superficial government form. The problem—the sacrifice of our spiritual life to a humanistic ideal—is the same in both the East and the West.

9
WHOSE ARE THE CHILDREN?

One of the basic rights of parents is the right to rear their
own children and to dictate the details of their children's
lives as long as they are under the parents' care. This right
has been challenged many times in history but perhaps
never so drastically as in socialistic societies. Part of the
doctrine of social determinism in the "gospel of Marx" is
that since the state is the great savior and benefactor of
society, it is in the best interests of everyone concerned if
the state controls the destinies of its children. Under
socialistic creeds, the children belong to the state.

In light of this view, a recent remark by a judge in Ohio
is especially interesting. According to the *CLA Defender*,
June 1978, Judge Angelo J. Gagliardo, the Cuyahoga
County Juvenile magistrate, said, " 'Children ... are not
pawns, they are not the property of parents!' Rather, he
insisted, they are wards of the state, and the court (meaning
Judge Gagliardo) would perform that which was in the best

interest of the children (as determined by Judge Gagliardo rather than by the parents)."

The writer of this article, Alan H. Grover, made the above observations in the process of a case involving a Mr. and Mrs. Tom Lippitt, who had chosen to educate their own children. It is one of scores of such cases in various states in which the right of parents to determine the course of their children's lives has been dramatically challenged by state agencies and courts.

Tom Lippitt is a very ordinary Ohio citizen who became upset with some left-wing comments published in a Cleveland newspaper in 1962. After he wrote his own answers to a series of letters to the editor, he became the subject of some abuse. This led to another letter to the editor and a growing involvement in conservative political affairs. He eventually joined the John Birch Society and ran for Congress three times as a candidate of the American Independent Party.

The Lippitts put their two daughters in private school when they reached school age. They became dissatisfied, however, when they discovered that the school used many of the textbooks they objected to in the public schools. They also found the private school "too permissive." Investigating other schools brought additional disappointments for these parents and they were finally able to find only one school which they felt reflected their philosophy and beliefs about the Bible. But it required an eighty-mile round trip each day, which was too much of a strain on their schedule and their aging family automobile. The Lippitts finally decided to start their own private school. Mrs. Lippitt had been certified by the Ohio Department of Education with competency in secondary English, French, Spanish, and German. She had had many years of teaching experience. As a professional educator and also the mother of the children, she felt well qualified to teach them. They opened the Martha I. Lippitt Christian Day School with the idea of educating their two daughters and others who might wish to attend.

This is where their plans ran counter to official state

policies, which assume that the only valid educator of children is the state, and that it must approve the existence of even private schools. Under this philosophy, parents are not competent to teach their own children. It is surprising how many people have arrived at this position. After a little over a century of publicly controlled education, it is almost universally believed. Most people see the imposing buildings, the great system, the flamboyant emphasis on athletics and extracurricular activities, and regard the state system as the only valid educator of children.

The first state board of education in this country came into being in 1837 in the state of Massachusetts. Many people saw the dangers and opposed the trend toward public education. But the movers in the field of education, inspired by the humanists, continued to push for a "free" public school system. Many parents did not cooperate. The enforced schedules often interrupted family priorities. Educators began to push for compulsory attendance laws, until by 1918 all of the states had adopted them. It had now become unlawful anywhere in the United States for children not to attend school.

Like so many other programs begun with good intentions, the enforced attendance laws have become sources of legitimate concern among Christian parents. They present a dilemma for people who want their children educated, but not according to humanistic standards. Roy W. Lowrie Jr., Executive Director of the National Christian School Education Association, writes in his little tract, "The Dilemma of Contemporary Education":

> The dilemma is this: Education has misplaced God as the cornerstone for life and is using man instead .... In recent years every major legal decision in education has gone against the place of God and the Bible.
>
> To illustrate, a first grade girl in Illinois brought the dilemma into focus for her parents. One day after school she asked her mother, "Mommy, if God is so important, why doesn't my teacher ever talk about Him in school?"

What do Christian parents do when the school entrusted with their children's education undermines the beliefs and morals of the parents? It is a problem not only for parents

but for Christian leaders as well. They find that a few
minutes in a Sunday school classroom each week cannot
compete with the constant challenges to the children's faith
in the secular classroom. The atheism and infidelity that
once affected the university campus alone have invaded the
kindergarten. This was the situation the Lippitts faced.
They did not want to send their children to a tax-supported
institution which would undo everything they had tried to
teach their children about God and His Bible.

Their small, new school was no casual, claptrap affair. It
operated in the family room of a fine home; the
surroundings were well arranged, comfortable, and
pleasant. Desks were provided.

In Ohio it is against the law to send children to an
unlicensed school. Parents who do so can be prosecuted
under either criminal or civil statutes. The criminal
statutes can result in imprisonment. Under civil
procedures, custody of the children can be turned over to
the welfare department. In this case, the state moved
against the parents from both directions. They had to face
two separate trials. It was the civil trial that Judge
Gagliardo heard. Although the Lippitts based their case on
First Amendment rights, claiming that they stood on their
religious convictions, Gagliardo refused to permit any
religious testimony to be entered into the proceedings. He
ordered the Lippitts to place their children in a public
school or a state-licensed private school. Failure to do so
would result in their children's being taken away.

In fear, this mother disappeared with her children. She
left a note for her husband: "The only answer is to leave and
run my Christian school underground as it is done in Soviet
Russia. Don't try to find me. I will watch the papers from
Cleveland in the main library in the city I am in to see if you
ever win this case, but I doubt it as we now have a dictator-
ship. Love, hastily, and take care of yourself.—Martha."

Tom Lippitt was jailed for contempt of court for failing
to carry out the orders of the court. He was released on bond
in a week, but his determined wife conducted her
underground school for her children for forty-nine

days in six different locations. Finally, on December 7,
Judge Gagliardo stayed the order for her arrest and the
couple was reunited. When the appellate court refused to
hear the case, Martha Lippitt was placed in jail and her
children were removed from their home. The evening news
on Cleveland television showed the mother and children
being carried bodily from the home.

As far as the state was concerned, those children, Amy
and Alice, did not belong to the parents or even to God. They
belonged to the state. It would be naive to think this was an
idea invented by the state of Ohio. It is a concept of the
socialistic philosophy that has somehow captivated the
American society, and the Lippitts are not the only ones
who have been persecuted for daring to think otherwise.

In Syracuse, New York, a fourteen-year-old girl was
removed from the home of her parents, the Rev. and Mrs.
James Roy. Both parents agreed that their daughter,
Shirley, needed a spanking. They explained to her why they
must take the disciplinary action, read the Bible to her, and
prayed with her. Then Roy spanked his daughter with a
light cedar shingle. Under the guise of children's rights,
the Welfare Department seized the child, placed her in the
home of foster parents with radically different religious
convictions, and refused to tell the parents where she was.

In Knox County, Ohio, criminal charges were brought
against Jim Olin because he had entered his daughter in an
Amish school. The Amish are permitted to operate
unlicensed schools under First Amendment considerations, but Jennifer Olin was not Amish and the state
ruled that it was against the law for her to attend. Again, it
was not left to the parents to make the decision. (This case is
important because it could result in a ruling that
Methodists, for instance, cannot send their children to a
Baptist school.)

Perhaps one of the most notable recent truancy cases
involved the Rev. Levi Whisner of Bradford, Ohio, pastor of
the Tabernacle Christian Church in Greenville. A few area
parents had decided to begin a Christian school. They were
from a variety of denominational backgrounds, but they

were united on cardinal points of Bible doctrine, including the necessity of the new birth, separation from the world, and discipleship. These parents were wary of the consequences to their children of the things they had seen in the public schools. They opened their small school in September 1974 with twenty-four pupils, an experienced teacher, a few teacher's aides, and Whisner as its principal.

Parents soon received truancy notices from local officials. Ohio requires all school-age children, except for the handicapped, to attend a school that "conforms to the minimum standards prescribed by the state board of education." The word "minimum" as used by Ohio officials is something of a misnomer. The "minimum standards" appear in a 150-page book, and some of them violate the religious convictions of the parents and school board. As in other cases of this type, the board of the tiny school realized after reading the standards that, if they were followed to the letter, their Christian school would be effectively converted into a counterpart of public schools. Whisner informed the state that their school could not comply. Prosecution began, and noted constitutional attorney William B. Ball was engaged by the parents to defend their case.

After much legal maneuvering, the parents were tried on May 7 and 8, 1974. Prior to this, a letter seeking a ruling out of court was never acknowledged by the state. Whisner was the first witness called by the defense. He outlined carefully the parents' religious convictions and the reasons they could not violate those convictions. They pleaded First Amendment rights. The pastor summed up his position under cross-examination:

> Lee G. Fry, state prosecutor: I am going to ask you, why did you not submit such a plan [as required by the minimum standard], Rev. Whisner?
>
> Whisner: After reading somewhat carefully the minimum standards program, I felt sincerely that this would constitute an agreement on our part to abide by, or conform to, the whole program here. It says here, to all in number 6, all standards. I didn't feel in my heart as a matter of conscience that we could conform to all standards.

The careful answer of this Ohio pastor is significant. Remember, the courts have decided that a religious conviction is a strong belief that one will not change, even under pressure. Had Whisner and the other parents agreed to the minimum standards, in violation of their religious beliefs, they could have placed themselves in a position where they could not, at a later time, defend themselves under the First Amendment. In order to come under First Amendment protection they had to resist the standards.

But something even more valuable was at stake—their convictions. Personal belief to the point of conviction is what this case was about. It is the gist of all cases in which people have to stand against unlawful and unrighteous regulations. In researching this type of case across the country, I expected to find some who were being merely foolish and stubborn. I expected to find some publicity-hunters. But such is not the case. If individuals like that are involved in such cases, I have not found them. In my estimation, these are people who are standing for their convictions at great personal cost.

One remarkable fact that comes out of these cases is that it is often other people in the *Christian* community who give these nonconformists their greatest opposition. When Levi Whisner took his stand, aside from that handful of parents, very few stood with him. Other pastors and Christian friends thought he was a reactionary, that he ought to give it up before he brought discredit upon other Christians in the community. This is part of the state's strategy in many of these cases. If a person can be branded in the community as a lawbreaker, a stubborn, unthinking malcontent, even other Christians will put pressure upon him to change.

The month of May dragged by with no decision in the Whisner case. June, July, and part of August came while this pastor and the people of his school pondered their fate. Finally, on August 16, 1974, they got word of the decision. They all faced jail sentences. They appealed, but lost in the appeals court on August 30, 1974; and a three-judge panel upheld the decision of the lower court in April 1975.

As the case began to attract statewide and then national attention, the stand that Whisner and his followers had taken began to pay off. Dr. Roy Thompson of the Christian Schools of Ohio (CSO) stepped in with help. Having seen the small band of determined Christians stand, many now began to lock arms and rally with them. "How much more could we do if many more would stand?" That was the nagging question that played with the thoughts of leaders such as Dr. Thompson, and many other concerned Fundamentalists. These leaders in Christian education in Ohio had been standing for years and had often been misunderstood for their stand. But the tiny, valiant band in Greenville was challenging the respect of a growing number of Ohioans. Their stand was later influential in leading the Rev. Jim Moody and his church in Canal Winchester, Ohio, to take a similar stand.

Conservative columnists began to bring out their ammunition. On July 3, 1975, Rus Walton wrote in his nationally syndicated column:

> Caesar is at it again! He's out busting heads and cracking down on liberty. He just will not put up with those who refuse to walk in lockstep with his program.
> This time he's taking out after a small band of fundamentalist Christians in Greenville, Ohio. Fifteen parents ... had the temerity to ... send their kids to a Christian school in that small town. He went after them full tilt; indicted them, hauled them into court, found them guilty, and fined them for their exercise of freedom. Hail, you lousy Caesar! Chalk up another score for the lions.
> And what of the Christians? What were their crimes? Wanting their children to be taught around moral values based on biblical truths. Placing their children in an academic environment polluted with "standards of modesty, sobriety, humility, prayerfulness and separation from the world."
> Horrors! What's this world coming to?

Dr. Max Rafferty featured the Tabernacle Christian School cause in his column dated Tuesday, August 19, 1975:

> Time: Now
> Plot: The church operates a private school for children of its congregation. Said school is nonaccredited by the state of

Ohio. Reason: It's against the Tabernacleans' religious
beliefs to have their school accredited by anyone except God.
So the public school Establishment in Ohio has proceeded
against twelve of the parents, charging them with violating
the compulsory education laws. They've been duly tried,
found guilty, and are now faced with jail.

Villains: The humorless, jealous, picky-nicky public
school Pecksniffs who started the agitation in the first place,
and the idiotic grand jury which then indicted the poor
parents in the second place.

Heroes: School principal Levi Whisner and his embattled
congregation.

Let us pause here to ask a few pregnant questions. Is
organized crime so rare in beautiful Ohio that grand juries,
judges and district attorneys have sufficient time hanging
heavy on their hands to enable them to browbeat God-
fearing parents for daring to educate their own children in
their own church school?

How about murders? Muggings? Bank stickups? . . . Are
there no drug pushers on the streets seducing the kids with
hell-power?

Oh, I know. The laws are on the books and must be
enforced. But any law which says that kids can't get their
education in their own church school has been nullified by
the . . . Supreme Court.

He went on in his column to explain that it is not a case of
children's suffering from a poor-quality education, because
it had been shown that the children at Tabernacle
Christian Schools excelled above others. Rafferty surmised
that it was precisely that the fundamentalist Christians in
Greenville espoused a square, rugged morality that was
unacceptable to the movers in modern public education. He
closed his column by saying, "Somebody in Ohio should
take a swamp-elm club to the meddlers. God is having a
tough enough time as it is these days without having His
schools 'accredited' by some team of languid bureaucrats
who have themselves confused with Him."

Rafferty writes as a seasoned observer on the
educational scene, having been Superintendent of Schools
of the state of California for a number of years. His column
deals almost exclusively with the current problems in the
field of education. And he has put his finger on a basic truth
that the general public has not discerned in these struggles:

it is a conflict of religious philosophy. Make no mistake
about it, the bedrock convictions of Bible-believers are the
number one enemy of the collectivistic, socialistic march of
our society. As long as people are free to educate their
children to believe the Bible, to look at the world as a God-
centered world, those children will not swallow the
doctrine that man is his own god and the state is the great
benefactor of the people.

It did not matter that the children at Tabernacle
Christian Schools were receiving a better education than
children in the public schools. The issue was not education.
The issue was this: who has the right to control the children,
the parents or the state? An article by Merle R. Hull in *The
Baptist Bulletin* underscored the issue:

> As with many others, however, this principle of the
> Scripture is under severe siege today. And more than we
> realize, the walls have already been breached. There is an
> increasing surge in the direction of taking responsibility for
> children away from the parents and putting it in the hands
> of "professionals."
> The revised Education Code, Ohio School Guide
> Compulsory Education Law, states: *"The natural rights of a
> parent to custody and control of their children are
> subordinate to the power of the state to provide for the
> education of children.* Laws providing for the education of
> children are *for the protection of the state itself"* [emphasis
> added].

The whole basis of the statist approach is that the state
knows best for the children, that the parents' rights are
subordinate to those of the state, and that the preservation
of the statist principle is absolutely dependent upon
destroying the traditional concept of the family and
making children the wards of the state.

Parents in America need to ask themselves if they are
ready for that. If that is what they want, that is what they
will get. Christians, in particular, will have to ask
themselves if they are going to stand with those who are
fighting for their rights to be lawful parents of their own
children, or if they are willing to surrender that ultimate
responsibility to the government.

Hull went on to say:

In Wisconsin relatively recent legislation has established a Child Placement Review Board affecting all institutions licensed by the state. This board essentially assumes the right to determine where children may be placed and for how long; it is no longer the parents' prerogative.

In Indiana the juvenile division of a welfare office informed a mother that she had no right to her sixteen-year-old boy. Furthermore, they informed this mother that if *they* allowed (note the assumption of authority) the boy to go with her, she was not to mention the church or God in the home again.

In Illinois a Christian parent was told by a high school department head that the school would determine the reading material given students and that if parents did not like it, they could transfer their children to a parochial school.

Basically, this is the issue in the famed West Virginia textbook controversy. Attention has centered on the violence involved and the textbook quotations. But behind all this is the question of whether parents have the right to determine what is being etched into the minds of their children.

We must ask ourselves how our public servants, paid with our tax dollars, ever got into the position of being "lords over God's heritage," the children. How did we give them the power to do it? Where did they assume that they had such authority? Where did they get such ideas?

I have tried to write with the trained eye of the journalist; and I believe those who have heard me preach around the country will say that I have tried not to be a paranoid, seeing persecutions, conspiracies, and Communists behind every rock and tree. But in seeing a devastating, organized effort to subvert the minds of children, we have some pretty good company.

Martin Luther said, "I am much afraid that schools will prove to be the great gates of Hell unless they diligently labor in explaining the Holy Scriptures, engraving them in the hearts of youth."

Theodore Roosevelt said, "To educate a man in mind and not in morals is to educate a menace to society."

Daniel Webster said, "Knowledge does not comprise all

which is contained in the large term of education. The feelings are to be disciplined; the passions are to be restrained; true and worthy motives are to be inspired; a profound religious feeling is to be instilled, and a pure morality inculcated under all circumstances. All this is comprised in education."

We believe that what Dr. Rushdoony said about the humanists (see chapter eight) is true. They are not fools. If you wanted to turn the wave of the future toward the philosophy of humanistic collectivism, where would you go? You would not start in the homes for the aged. Nor would you waste much time with the hard-working middle class, already set in its ways. You would find the largest possible audience of young people, those who would be the leaders and opinion-makers of the future. And where are they to be found? They are to be found in the largest captive audience in the country, the compulsory public education system. If I wanted to spread the gospel of Jesus Christ to the widest, most impressionable audience in the nation, that's where I would go. But I cannot go there. It is against the law to preach the gospel in the public schools of America. But it is not against the law to preach the doctrine of atheistic collectivism. In fact, that is the only "gospel" that can lawfully be preached in the schools of the land.

Earnest Christians have found a way to provide a godly education for their own children and other children whose parents will make the financial sacrifices necessary for them to attend. But the humanistic forces in education are not content for us to do even that. They have shown that they are not going to be satisfied until this threat to their plans and ambitions is stamped out. And thus, the battle lines are drawn between a huge, public-financed system with great power, and a small but determined minority whose philosophy of life is diametrically opposed to the humanistic philosophy. The two of them cannot exist in the same society without one of them coming out the victor.

I have before me a letter from Senator Orrin G. Hatch, a fine, conservative senator who fought courageously to save U.S. ownership of the Panama Canal. He asks some pertinent questions:

Do you believe that children should have the right to sue their parents for being "forced" to attend church?

Should children be eligible for minimum wage if they are asked to do household chores?

Do you believe that children should have the right to choose their own family?

As incredible as they might sound, these are just a few of the new "children's rights laws" that could become a reality under a new United Nations program if fully implemented by the Carter Administration!

Senator Hatch goes on to describe how the same anti-family forces which fought for the International Women's Year, mentioned briefly earlier in this book, are sponsoring an International Children's Year in 1979. Nothing is so likely to arouse feelings of goodwill as planning a special year for children. Almost everybody likes children.

But what are their goals? According to Hatch, they include abortion, government-supervised family planning, legalization of homosexual marriages in which the "couple" could have children by adoption or artificial insemination, an "Equal Rights Amendment" for children, and government takeover of all responsibilities concerning children.

It is clear that these pressures arise from international sources. One does not have to believe any of the conspiracy theories to believe that. One has only to look at the plain facts. Why should international forces seeking to advance the worldwide doctrines of dialectical materialism risk nuclear war if they can accomplish their ends so much more effectively another way? The bomb that has been dropped on our society is not a nuclear bomb. It is a philosophical bomb.

Confronted with such a well-financed, determined effort, most of us feel helpless. What can we do? Perhaps in the long run, getting involved in the political process will accomplish some things. But many of the men who are already in places of office, dedicated to turning the thing around, also feel helpless. They are desperately in need of help from the people of the nation who share their philosophy.

My appraisal is that the only thing that can save us is a revival which will bring the direct intervention of God. But how can that come about? In II Chronicles 7:14, we read, "If my people, which are called by my name, shall humble themselves, and pray, and seek my face, and turn from their wicked ways; then will I hear from heaven, and will forgive their sin, and will heal their land."

Among the things found in that formula for restoration are turning from our wicked ways and having our sin forgiven. What are our wicked ways? One of them is saying we believe a Book that we are not living by. We have neglected to rear our children in the ways of God, turning that responsibility over to a secular institution. Rather than taking a firm stand for what is right, regardless of the consequences, we have yielded to pressure, betrayed our convictions, and let the bureaucrats and politicians have their day. Our rights have been taken away and we have not stirred.

We have wanted "our share" of the worthless money issuing forth from our printing presses, regardless of the cost to us in personal conviction. We have let our local leaders sell our souls for federal money.

We have rolled over and gone to sleep while militant, dedicated zealots have virtually captured every level of influence and power in the country. The Supreme Court kicked the Bible out of the schools; we kicked the Bible out of our homes. Affluence, worldliness, pleasure-mad pursuits, and apathy rule our churches.

And when one of us occasionally wakes up and wants to do something, our attitude is, "I surely wish he would go back to sleep. He's going to make it awfully hard on the rest of us."

But it is not all bad. Here is one optimist who is unwilling to shrug his shoulders and say, "It's all over for us. Better salvage what little we can and try to stay alive." I believe it can be turned around, but to do it, God's people must stand. Oh, I am not talking about making a lot of noise and taking our placards into the street and getting out the vote. Those things may be necessary, but God reads our hearts. I do not think anything but a willingness to stand against every kind of unrighteous force, whether on the government level or not, even if it means imprisonment or death, will avail for us now. If some brave ones will stand, others will stand.

At first, Levi Whisner and his brave little band stood virtually alone. But they stood. They stood until the CSO took up their cause. They stood until Rafferty and Walton raised a banner in their defense. Finally, on December 8, 1975, an estimated ten thousand people gathered on the steps of the state capitol in mass support for the Tabernacleans and another small group in Canal Winchester, as well as others involved in the fight.

The politicians responded. Governor Rhodes said, "I fully support the right of every parent in Ohio rallying at the State House for legislation supporting their church-sponsored schools .... The church school is the last bastion of discipline in our school system."

Representative Sam Speck said, "I share your concern." He then invited parents in his constituency to meet him in his office.

Representative Harry Malott told the crowd, "I am with you as long as I am in the General Assembly."

On July 28, 1976, the Ohio Supreme Court overturned the opinions of lower courts and ruled in favor of the Tabernacle Christian Schools. A great victory was won.

But the state of Ohio is still going after others as you read these pages. The humanists are not dead. A long, hard fight is ahead.

10

THE "IMPERIAL" IRS?

Already, there are 33 federal agencies and some 400 bureaus and subagencies operating more than 1,000 consumer-oriented programs. The cost of all this regulation has been estimated at $2,000 per family per year—a staggering $130 billion altogether.

Recently a New York Times-CBS survey revealed that 58 percent of those polled agreed with a statement that government has gone too far in the direction of regulation of business and interference with the free enterprise system. That percentage is up sharply from the 42 percent recorded in 1964.

The above wire-service release is just one of many heralding the current restlessness among U.S. citizens concerning taxation. Recently there have been some controversial tax reform efforts: California's Proposition 13; the constitutional amendment in Tennessee which ties government spending to the inflation rate; and the current efforts by the National Tax Limitation Committee, headed by the brilliant economist Milton Friedman, seeking a similar amendment to the U.S. Constitution. Citizens are beginning to hope for some relief from the big spenders in government. And it is about time. But the grassroots surge toward cutting government costs may contain a hidden peril for churches.

Many people, even conservatives, are beginning to turn a jaundiced eye toward nonprofit, tax-exempt organizations, including churches. The danger is that as proposed tax reforms cause the federal money supply to dwindle, nonprofit organizations may be made to prove that they qualify for tax-exempt status by adhering to restrictive guidelines imposed by federal agencies. If you have laws and regulations on the books requiring nonprofit and religious organizations to qualify for nonprofit status, you have a situation that multiplies red tape, government meddling, and endless reports that must be filed by churches. There is also the threat of endless litigation.

Nothing is more powerful than the heavy hand of federal intervention in local-level enterprises. This has been borne out by the "federal money" clout exercised in local educational circles. It works this way: The federal government takes our money with the promise that they will give us back in services that part not absorbed by the cost of administering the funds. We get back about two-thirds, but we do not get it back until we meet certain conditions. It is our money. We paid it in taxes. But now when it comes back to us, we cannot have it until we meet certain conditions.

But that is not the worst of it. You would think local authorities would have a choice, but they don't. Regulations handed down by government officials are the law of the land. They must be followed. The problem is that it costs a tremendous amount of money to implement these requirements. For instance, a great part of our energy problem and a lot of the cost of education could be taken care of if local school boards did not have to bus children across town to achieve the plans of the social reformers. The federally required programs cost tremendous amounts of money and put local governments in a bind where they must depend upon "federal" money to survive. But the money comes back to us with strings that turn into chains.

The agency charged with the primary responsibility for collecting "federal" money is the Internal Revenue Service. There are few organizations on earth more powerful than the IRS. One reason for this is that they make many of their own ground rules without the consent of elected legislators. Another reason is that the roles are reversed in legal matters pertaining to their collection of our money. This country's system of jurisprudence assumes that the accused is innocent until proven guilty. The court bears the burden to prove any wrongdoing. But in IRS matters, it is up to the accused to prove that he has not "cheated" the government. We wonder sometimes who is cheating.

I remember being audited for the third time. My income was just slightly above the designated poverty level. As I was trying to show how certain travel expenses were justified, the young lady from the IRS told me, "These deductions are money the government is giving you. You have to show why they are justified." I replied that I had always thought it was the other way around. I told her that I had the impression she was *working for me*. That only made matters worse.

The embattled taxpayer has to pay for the bookkeeping, account for every penny he makes, and justify every deduction. If he does not measure up to IRS expectations, his property can be confiscated, his bank account can be raided, and he can be put into prison. Of course, he has legal recourse. But he is dealing with a very powerful adversary.

Now imagine that churches are made to qualify for tax exemption. At the present time, if a church is chartered under its state as a religious nonprofit institution, or even if it is simply organized as a church, it is considered exempt. But if churches have to start filing forms to show that they qualify, a number of things can happen. The most dangerous thing is that the federal government will start laying down guidelines that must be followed in order to obtain the exemption. That is government control of the church. Whenever bureaucrats start snooping into the affairs of every church in the U.S., examining their records and monitoring their affairs, freedom of religion in this country has been effectively circumvented.

There is such an IRS regulation on the books now, effective as of 1976. It just hasn't been enforced yet.

The scenario for the future, according to some reports, is something like this: the government will begin to move on the churches to qualify. Those who do not or cannot will lose their tax exemption privileges. That simply means if a little country church has a $10,000 per year income its contributors cannot claim tax exemption and in extreme cases the church itself may have to pay taxes on its income, just as a business does.

Another, more ominous step is envisioned according to these unconfirmed reports. At some point in the future, one of the requirements for qualification for tax exemption could be that churches belong to a "recognized" body such as the World Council of Churches. Another requirement may be that churches demonstrate a certain pattern of integration in order to achieve tax-exempt status. If that happens, discrimination according to sex will not be allowed; churches will have to have women preachers and officers, even if their convictions oppose it. And religious freedom will be a thing of the past.

This may seem to be a farfetched likelihood, but the IRS has given recent dramatic evidence of how far they intend to go. They have set out to make private schools, even church schools, "prove" they are not segregationist institutions in order to remain tax-exempt. A proposed IRS ruling, already in the *Federal Register*, has been hotly contested. Dr. Paul A. Kienel, director of the Association of Christian Schools International, reported in *Christian School Comment* what has become well-known to Christian educators:

> On August 22, 1978, Jerome Kurtz, U.S. Commissioner of the Internal Revenue Service, shocked the Christian school world with his Proposed Internal Revenue Procedures On Private Tax-Exempt Schools. He said, in effect, that all

church-sponsored and independent religious schools located within a community where there is a public school desegregation program are guilty of racial discrimination. This also applies to any school outside a desegregated community if the government so rules. These schools are guilty, Mr. Kurtz said, if they were founded after the federal desegregation in 1957; or they are guilty if they were founded earlier but have had a substantial enrollment increase since the desegregation program began. They are guilty not on the basis of whether or not they practice discrimination, but on the basis that the school came into existence or increased its enrollment after 1957. By their very existence they are guilty!

It is very sad that this, along with the ruling by Ray Marshall, has come in the administration of a President who professes to be "born again."

The school of which I am president, Berean Academy, has never had a racial policy. From the beginning we made the choice to open our doors to all. But under this ruling we would have to prove that fact in order to remain tax-exempt. And what would we have to do to prove it? Here are the regulations as they appeared in the *Federal Register:*

A school will be considered to be racially discriminatory to minority students unless the school can demonstrate:
Section 4.02
  1. Actual enrollment of minority students such that the percentage of minority students enrolled in the school is at least 20 percent of the percentage of the minority school age population in the community, or
  2. Operation in good faith on a racially nondiscriminatory basis as evidenced by the existence of at least four of the five factors set forth in Section 4.03, infra. Only in rare and unusual circumstances will a school be operated in good faith on a nondiscriminatory basis if the school does not enroll some minority students.
Section 4.03 Operation in good faith on a racially nondiscriminatory basis. The following five factors evidence operation in good faith on a nondiscriminatory basis—
  1. Availability of and granting of scholarships or other financial assistance on a significant basis to minority students.
  2. Active and vigorous minority recruitment programs, such as contacting prospective minority students and organizations from which prospective minority

students could be identified.
3. An increasing percentage of minority student enrollment.
4. Employment of minority teachers or professional staff.
5. Other substantial evidence of good faith, including evidence of a combination of lesser activities, such as—
    (a) Continued and meaningful advertising programs beyond the requirements of Revenue Procedure 75-50 [this requirement included the provision that private schools place ads in local papers advertising that they are nondiscriminatory], or contracts with minority leaders inviting applications from minority students.
    (b) Significant efforts to recruit minority teachers.
    (c) Participation with integrated schools in sports, music, and other events or activities.
    (d) Making school facilities available to outside, integrated civic or charitable groups.
    (e) Special minority-oriented curriculum or orientation programs [such as black history].
    (f) Minority participation in the founding of the school or current minority board members.

The proposed ruling stirred up a storm of protest. Thousands of letters reached Commissioner Kurtz's office daily. Among them was a letter dated October 6, 1978, and signed by the Honorable Larry P. McDonald, James M. Collins and 68 other U.S. congressmen. It said in part:

> Selection based on fair and unbigoted standards is a goal for which we hope all men strive, men being used in the generic sense. Guidance of this ideal, however, is not a governmental function. Government should govern the basic freedom in which we make selections. Other institutions such as the family and the church are the ones who have been given the province of guiding such selections in this Western Society, and should continue to provide this guidance.
>
> For the government to have the authority to engineer its interpretation of equality is for government to become the most powerful discriminator of all.

Dr. David C. Innes, pastor of Hamilton Square Baptist Church in San Francisco, wrote:

> I am writing in a fivefold capacity: as the pastor of a

prominent Baptist church, as the president of an Association of Churches that covers northern California and Western Nevada, as a member of the Board of Trustees of a Theological Seminary, as a member of the Board of Trustees of a church-related Christian School, and as the father of four children all of whom are presently attending school.

Lest my remarks be construed as having racial overtones, let me clarify that the Christian School on whose Board of Trustees I serve has a student body composed of over 50% minority students, and a faculty of over 30% minority teachers. Blacks, Spanish Americans, Filipinos, Chinese, Arabs, and others are represented. Our seminary has a minority student enrollment of over 30%.

Writing in behalf of the organizations which he represented, Dr. Innes stated his objections to the proposed regulation:

This will preclude the possibility of the establishment of any Christian School for the following reasons:

1. Any church-related school by the necessity of its nature as a church-related school will reflect the racial character of the congregation of the church, not necessarily the community.
2. Church-operated schools normally operate on a shoestring financially and do not have the capacity to grant scholarships on a significant basis to anyone; nor can they afford vigorous recruitment programs or the continued and meaningful advertising programs demanded by the proposed regulation. They have neither the money nor the personnel necessary to meet these demands.
3. Christian Schools are not able to recruit students and faculty in the sense required by the proposed regulation without destroying the very nature of their ministry. Only those who are fully supportive of the Church's doctrinal beliefs and standards of conduct qualify as prospects for enrollment. This severely limits the capacity of any Christian School in its enrollment of students or hiring of faculty.
4. Churches with a related Christian school are usually crowded and very limited in their facilities. The facilities are used by many different organizations that function within the program and the life of the church. Granting the use of the facilities to any outside organization would normally be out of the question.

5. The basic assumption that *all* Christian Schools in a
certain area are established for the distinct purpose of
"fleeing integrated schools" places an inordinate and
totally unjustifiable burden of proof on any church. To
insist that churches must legally justify their
ministries before they can operate them is not only
unwarranted government meddling in church
affairs, but also highly oppressive and restrictive.

It is to be considered tragic that a governmental agency
can use public funds to suppress, harass, and intimidate our
churches whose financial capacity to fight the necessary
legal battles is limited to the extent of being virtually
nonexistent. Truly, the power to tax is the power to destroy!

The IRS move is not new; it began in 1970 when the
agency decided, without any congressional action, to
remove deductability status from private schools that
maintain racially discriminatory enrollment policies.
Whether or not this is constitutional remains to be seen. In a
case involving Bob Jones University in 1974, the Supreme
Court dismissed an injunction on the strength of the Anti-
Injunction Act which prevents a tax-exempt organization
from suing to prevent the IRS from collecting taxes. The
Supreme Court has not acted on any related cases since that
dismissal. The constitutional issue remains dormant as far
as the High Court is concerned.

In the September 1978 issue of the *Non-Profit
Organization Tax Letter*, an entry reveals that the IRS
often has contempt not only for the freedom of churches,
but for courts as well:

The IRS is proposing to issue a published ruling
indicating that it does not follow the *Oklahoma Cattlemen's*
case. One of the statements made by the IRS in the ruling to
be published is as follows:
"The Service will not follow the decision in *Oklahoma
Cattlemen's*. Although we believe the services rendered by
providing group insurance plans are sufficient ...
"The court in *Oklahoma Cattlemen's* seems to have
reasoned that providing group insurance is related to the
exempt purposes ...."

In other words, there was a court decision against IRS
procedure, but the IRS simply chose not to abide by it, to
ignore it! And their decision was based upon their own

interpretation of what the court meant. The *Tax Letter's* comment is significant:

It is interesting to note that the IRS and Justice Department have followed their long used position when a case arises in a Federal District Court and the government loses. They merely don't appeal and don't follow it [the court's decision]. This has been exemplified recently with the threat of the Justice Department Tax Division to dismiss a test case pending in the Court of Claims and try another case in a Federal District Court. Of course, if the government loses in a particular Federal District Court, they will not appeal and the case then will not be a national precedent (applicable to all taxpayers) as in the case in the U.S. Court of Claims. This is called in law school "forum shopping" or in less academic circles, it is called "unethical" or "cheating." This is what the government is doing in the Oklahoma Cattlemen's case.

This report indicates that not only will churches be financially unprepared to fight the big, meddling IRS, but they have no guarantee that their case will ever get anywhere in the courts.

An editorial in the *Washington Star*, August 29, 1978, said:

Thus the IRS "revenue procedure" for private schools, designed to make trouble for practices no one defends in principle [e.g., arbitrary discrimination], extends the taxing power to erode another realm of private choice and conduct: choice and conduct which, however deplorable or wrongheaded some may think it, once went unchallenged.

"The right to be wrong" used to be considered an important right. It involved not only the freedom to say or *think* what did not meet with majority approval, but also freedom to associate, even study, in settings disapproved by a majority.

No longer, it appears. If the IRS has its way in using the tax weapon on private schools, you can bid the latter assumption farewell. And prepare for the next stage of IRS imperialism, too.

Nobody who knows the situation seriously believes that the issue is segregation. The issue is money and control. And once again, the Christians of the United States of America are faced with the sobering question: what do we do with an unlawful law which threatens the basic foundation on which we build our whole lives, our religious convictions?

How many of us would continue to support our churches if our gifts were no longer exempt from taxation? Would we still stand? What will happen when the IRS knows everything about our churches? What kind of breaches of freedom are involved when we have to file reports concerning everything about our ministries? Can churches afford it? How will churches withstand the pressure put upon them to maintain the same policies of nondiscrimination now forced upon public agencies? How long would it be before such restrictions force the Bible-believing church to go underground?

These questions affect not only the churches which presently operate private schools. They affect every church, every pastor, every religious body in the country. Our faith is on trial.

11
WHAT IS A "CHARITABLE" INSTITUTION?

The reasoning behind certain actions taken by the IRS in recent years goes something like this. Whenever something becomes "public policy," they reason, it is, in effect, the law of the land. If an institution purporting to be a bona fide nonprofit or other tax-exempt organization maintains internal policies affecting the public that run counter to "public policy," it loses its legitimate privilege of tax exemption. This is the logical outgrowth of the philosophy that government is the only true provider of the people. As such, it must police any organization that threatens that role.

Tax exemption is a privilege granted by government benevolence. Tax-exempt organizations, it is reasoned, should exist for the public welfare. If such an organization does not conform to "public policy," it is evident, to the IRS at least, that it does not exist for the "public good." Under this reasoning, it ceases to be a charitable organization, and it becomes the duty of government to take away the tax-exempt privileges of the institution in question.

The IRS scored a major victory in *Goldsboro Christian Schools, Inc.* v. *United States* in 1977. Goldsboro Christian Schools maintained an admissions policy that totally excluded blacks. This, it was said, violated "public policy," and the school lost its tax-exempt status.

In *Goldsboro*, the court relied heavily on a case involving a commercial organization in *Tank Truck Rentals* v. *Commissioner* in 1958. In that case, the taxpayer had incurred some fines for violating the state penal code. The firm sought to claim the payment of these fines as a deduction. The court ruled against the plaintiff, finding that to allow deductions for the payment of fines would be against "public policy" in that it would encourage violations of penal statutes by allowing these deductions, and would, furthermore, take the "sting" out of the penalty. In using this as a precedent in *Goldsboro*, the court equated *deductions* and *exemptions* and applied the principle of "public policy" to both of them.

It is important to see that laws are made by both the legislative and judicial processes. "Public policy" limitation is a principle created by judicial process in the courts. This is the principle underlying the proposed IRS guidelines for determining the tax-exempt status for private schools (see chapter ten).

With this background, a court decision was rendered in U.S. District Court in Columbia, South Carolina, on December 26, 1978, by the Honorable Robert F. Chapman. The case involved Bob Jones University, which had earlier been denied injunctive relief against the IRS in the U.S. Supreme Court because of the Anti-Injunctive Act (see chapter ten). Although the University has maintained an open admissions policy since 1975, the IRS had revoked its tax-exempt status because it did not approve of the University's biblically-based policy against interracial dating and marriage within the student body. This time, the U.S. District Court ruled in favor of the University. The decision, if upheld, has broad ramifications in the battle currently being waged by Christian ministries in the arena of religious freedom in the United States.

Judge Chapman found some serious discrepancies in the government's arguments about "public policy," about its definition of a "charitable" organization, about whether the IRS has any business trying to determine such things at all, and about the findings in the Goldsboro case itself.

The court established the fact that Bob Jones University is a religious institution. This finding is of great importance in current litigation among private Christian schools and other institutions, such as children's homes, because the tendency of government has been to separate educational and other so-called secular functions from "religious" church ministries, giving them separate consideration. Bob Jones University does not claim to be a church but a religious educational institution. Judge Chapman found that, as a religious institution, the University was entitled to tax-exempt status regardless of the fact that it also served an educational purpose.

In current policy concerning private Christian schools, the Department of Labor under Ray Marshall has decreed that the educational function of a church ministry is a secular function and therefore subject to taxation. In the opinion of the court in *Bob Jones University* v. *United States of America*, however, this is a false distinction. The finding was based not on a mere claim to religious conviction but on examination of the practices of the University. The court concluded by the University's unwavering adherence that it was practicing a convictional belief. In the words of the court, "At some point in scrutinizing actions surrounding the practice of a religion, a distinction must be made between *actions related to a particular religious belief* and *the actual practice* of the belief itself" (emphasis added).

There is an implication here that a person can act in relation to a claimed belief, and still not consistently practice the belief itself. In this case, it was found that Bob Jones University practiced its convictions:

> The plaintiff is dedicated to the teaching and propagation of its fundamentalist religious beliefs. Everything taught at

plaintiff is taught according to the Bible. Although students may be exposed to theories that are contrary to Biblical scripture, plaintiff's teachers instruct them to disregard these theories and teach the Bible's literal language as being the only true account. The cornerstone of plaintiff institution is Christian religious indoctrination, not isolated academics ... in every instance where literature or philosophy vary from the "word of god" as set forth in the Bible .... Every teacher ... is required to be a "born again" Christian .... The institution does not permit dancing, card playing, the use of tobacco, movie-going ....

An abundance of evidence showing the University's consistent practice of its convictions was presented and accepted as fact by the Court. Its consistency over the years paid off in establishing a case for the policy in question, the forbidding of interracial dating, as being a logical outgrowth of genuinely held religious convictions.

In the eyes of the IRS, this internal policy revealed that this Christian university was discriminatory and therefore not entitled to tax exemption. The argument of the IRS was summarized by the court:

"The reconsideration and revocation of plaintiff's (BJU) exempt status stems from a decision by the IRS to construe S501 (C) (3) as requiring religious and educational organizations to be charitable in nature. Defendant contends the legislative intent behind this exemption section was to afford exemptions only to those organizations that could be considered charitable under common law and such law precludes an organization which violates clearly declared federal public policy from being considered charitable."

The IRS, the defendant in this case, also argued that the judicial sector had created a construction of S501 (c) (3) that had not heretofore been recognized.

The IRS argued that Bob Jones University disqualified itself as an educational institution under the statute because of its "discriminatory" internal rules. In commenting on that, the court found that the institution did not have to qualify as an *educational* entity since it had already qualified as a *religious* entity. The statute in question, S501 (c) (3) reads, in part:

(d) *Exempt Purposes*—(1) *In general.*
(i) An organization may be exempt as an organization described in section 501 (c) (3) if it is organized and operated exclusively for one or more of the following purposes:
  (a) Religious,
  (b) Charitable,
  (c) Scientific,
  (d) Testing for public safety,
  (e) Literary,
  (f) Educational, or
  (g) Prevention of cruelty to children or animals.

Each of these congressionally-mandated functions was originally considered sufficient for tax exemption purposes. But the IRS was contending that "charitable" included all the others, and that if other functions were operating contrary to public policy they were, in fact, not "charitable" institutions. Judge Chapman did not see it their way. In fact, he found their interpretation to be quite sinister. After establishing that the University was exempt under the restrictive clause of the First Amendment, he commented, "In addition, the Court discerns that the construction of S501 (c) (3) advocated and applied by the defendant (IRS) in this case seriously risks violation of the Establishment Clause of the First Amendment."

Remember, the First Amendment says, in part, that Congress shall make no law respecting an establishment of religion or prohibiting the free exercise thereof.

The court in this case found that IRS policies were not only restrictive in nature, but there was a danger that the government would, in fact, be showing a tendency to *establish a religion!* The importance of this thought in the current struggle for religious freedom can hardly be overestimated. But let the court speak for itself:

> Conflict with the Establishment Clause lurks within defendant's construction of the exemption provision because defendant puts no limit on its application. All religious organizations, such as plaintiff, are to be denied tax exemptions unless the IRS has judged the organization's purposes and practices to be in line with expressed federal policy. Under the government's reading of the statute, only those religious organizations whose purposes and practices

are in harmony with those of the federal government will be granted an exemption. To preserve its tax exemption, a church or other religious organization, such as plaintiff, would have to make sure it stayed in step with federal public policy.

That is, of course, what religious freedom advocates have been saying all along. Whenever the government tries to describe or define the limits of a religious ministry in any way it, in effect, establishes an official religion because the government reserves the right of approval. That is true in cases of licensure, taxation, and in every other area in which Christian ministries are being threatened. Misguided people within the Christian movement who have been arguing that to follow blindly anything the government demands is to "render unto Caesar the things that are Caesar's" need to beware! This court decision takes issue with that opinion and argues that there is a sinister danger lurking behind current government efforts to curtail bona fide Christian work! Or, as the court decision said:

> The application of the law, in the manner which defendant construes it, results in the government favoring those churches that adhere to federal policy .... Although the purpose of the government's construction of S501 (C) (3) may be considered secular in nature in that it promotes federal public policy, a primary effect is the inhibition of those religious organizations whose policies are not coordinated with declared national policy and the advancement of those religious groups that are in tune with federal public policy .... The unavoidable effect is the law's tending toward the establishment of the approved religions.

The court decision went on to note that to follow this policy would be to involve the government in having to "monitor continually" all religious works in order to ascertain their exempt status. The result would be, the court said, "an unlawful entanglement" between the state and religion.

The court also concluded that for the IRS to force the interpretation "charitable" upon each of the stated purposes originally intended by Congress to warrant exemption is to wrest the statute's original clear, unambiguous meaning. For an organization to be religious means it can stand alone on that basis and does not have to prove to the IRS or other government agencies that it is "charitable."

The U.S. District Court in Columbia also took exception to the findings in *Goldsboro*. The court found that the assumed connection between a *deduction* by a commercial fund and an *exemption* claimed by a religious institution was not called for. Establishing a connection based on *Tank Truck Rentals* v. *Commissioner* required a deliberate straining of language and law. The government had argued in *Tank Truck* that to permit the deduction was to encourage the breaking of the law. Applying that to *Goldsboro* and *Bob Jones*, the government contended that to grant tax-exempt status to such institutions would be to encourage segregation and discrimination. Judge Chapman's court opinion said, "To the contrary, permitting tax-exempt status to plaintiff does not so act as to encourage plaintiff to discriminate on the basis of race. Plaintiff's racial views result from sincerely held religious beliefs. Regardless of plaintiff's tax status, its religious beliefs remain immutable."

Once again, we are confronted with the power of an unchanging conviction. The government had put pressure upon this Christian institution, and it had refused to yield, even at great cost. Losing its tax-exempt status had cost Bob Jones University thousands of dollars in contributions, but its convictions had remained unchanged. The court also held that even if a taxpayer violates "public policy," that does not, in itself, call for his tax-exempt status to be removed. According to the 1966 *Commissioner* v. *Tellier* case, it is not the task of the IRS to determine wrongdoing, but simply to determine net worth and collect taxes: "We start with the proposition that the federal income tax is a tax on net income, not a sanction against wrongdoing. That principle has been firmly imbedded in the tax statute from the beginning. One familiar facet of the principle is the truism that the statute does not concern itself with the lawfulness of the income that it taxes."

In Judge Chapman's opinion, the *Commissioner* v. *Tellier* ruling renders some IRS policy null and void:

> "The defendant's blanket policy announcements in Revenue rulings and Procedures 71-447, 72-54, 75-50, and 75-231, that it will deny tax-exempt status to organizations which racially discriminate, but otherwise qualify under S501 (c) (3), constitute a use by the IRS of the federal tax law as a sanction for what it considers a wrongdoing, or its idea of proper social conduct of persons of different races, *uses of the Code prohibited by the Supreme Court*" [emphasis added].

This judge is telling the IRS to quit playing policeman and go back to its task of collecting taxes. Indeed, any kind of investigative activity by the agency against citizens is unconstitutional. The Fourth Amendment says, "The right of the people to be secure in their persons, houses, papers, and effects, against unreasonable searches and seizures, shall not be violated; and no warrants shall issue, but upon probable cause, supported by oath or affirmation, and particularly describing the place to be searched, and the persons or things to be seized . . . ."

Under present IRS policy and law, the IRS can determine that you owe a certain amount, and an agent can walk into a bank where you have money, write out a check, sign your name and initial it with his initials, and confiscate your money! No wonder many people are worried about the power of this agency. The court in *Bob Jones* was concerned about the proportions to which IRS power might grow:

> In addition, the Court is concerned by the many dangers inherent in defendant's interpretation that exemptions may be revoked for violations of federal public policy. Federal public policy is constantly changing. When can something be said to become federal public policy? Who decides? With a change of federal public policy, the law would change without congressional action—a dilemma of constitutional proportions. Citizens could no longer rely on the law of S501 (c) (3) as it is written, but would then rely on the IRS to tell them what it had decided the law to be for that particular day. Our laws would change at the whim of some nonelected IRS personnel producing bureaucratic tyranny.

The court was also troubled about the tendency of the IRS to decide who was benefiting the public and who was a menace to it. This was hidden in the arguments and policies of the agency. They presumed to have the power to determine when an organization was operating for "public benefit." Their test of this was simple. If an organization was operating in disharmony with "public policy" then it was evident that the organization was not operating for the "public benefit."

There is no greater danger inherent in the insidious philosophy of statism. The all-powerful state is the only legitimate provider of public benefit and it must monitor the activities of its citizens and organizations in order to determine if they are in tune with state policies. If they are not, they are considered a menace rather than a benefactor to society and are, in turn, suppressed by government agencies. It is this kind of reasoning that led to the elimination of millions of Christians in Russia, China, North Korea, and other parts of the world. It is a most sinister and powerful threat to the church in the United States. While the judge in *Bob Jones* may not agree with my appraisal, he did nevertheless have something to say about that kind of thinking:

> The Court considers defendant's logic on this point as somewhat of a nonsequitur, seemingly stemming from its confusion of the terms "public policy" and "public benefit." The two are not synonymous. Public policy is many faceted, one facet of which is that society may provide relief from taxation to those organizations, such as plaintiff religious organization, which are of benefit to the public. The good resulting to the public from these groups depends upon the fulfillment of their purposes. Because one of these organizations may have, in an area of its operations, engaged in conduct that might not have been completely in line with some other aspect of public policy does not automatically mean the public no longer benefits from the organization. Defendant seems to imply that a change in plaintiff's policies to conform to defendant's guidelines would transform the religious organization from one that did not benefit the public into one that did, although the function and purposes of plaintiff remain unchanged throughout.

I salute Judge Chapman and his court for their insight and clear interpretation of the actions of the IRS. It is our prayer that some of the victories won in this case may encourage many of the men now engaged in the fight for religious freedom and provide the basis for yet other victories.

Although we may be sure that the advocates of collectivism will not give up easily, this court decision reveals that with prayer, conviction, and a firm stand, victory can be won.

12

WHAT IS "COMPELLING INTEREST"?

One of the problems facing us in the church-state conflict is to arrive at a point at which we can draw the line between legitimate government interests and transgressions of religious freedom under the First Amendment. In other words, how much right does government have under our system to interfere in the affairs of religion? Does the state have any legitimate interest in the church? Can church and state exist in the same society without any overlap at all?

More specifically, should government control the right of churches to purchase land and build buildings under such provisions as zoning laws and building codes? Does the state have the right to force children to go to school even in church schools? Does the state have the right to enforce certain minimal standards of curriculum and teachers' qualifications? How about fire, health, and safety standards? Should the state exercise control over churches in these areas? If so, how much control? These are some of the hard questions being considered in courts across America today.

This chapter is being written in a room in The Ole Copper Inn, between Ducktown and Copper Hill, Tennessee. I come here to write every once in a while. The place is a rarity. The two small towns look like they are still in a previous era. Small stores and cafes belie the presence of Lincoln Continentals and huge trucks. The copper-colored hills are dotted with old farmhouses and neat, time-weathered barns. The drive here itself is refreshing. From Chattanooga, the road takes you along the banks of the rushing Ocoee River, past rocky cliffs which insulate the motorist from the technological age around him. The towering Smokies lie just ahead.

I got out my camera and drove up the back roads around Ducktown today, taking pictures of old sheds and barns in the hope that some day my schedule would give me time to paint some of them. Occasionally, small white signs would give directions to nearby churches, with names like "Turtletown Baptist Church." The nostalgia of a simpler day of little country churches, of simple people who want just to be left alone to carry on their occupations and rear their children, refreshed my mind. But I knew all the time that no mere sentimental journey could ever bring back the past in which people for the most part lived and died and never once encountered anything like bureaucratic guidelines for their lives.

Most of us have accepted the idea that the world is too complicated for that now. As a rule, little country churches are not seen as threats. But faith has taken on more cosmopolitan proportions. We live in the media age in which evangelists can raise millions through their television programs. Anytime anyone can handle millions of dollars, the government becomes intensely interested. And we live in the age of rising cultist influence.

The case of the Jonestown mass suicide was fresh in my mind. It is among the most macabre happenings in the history of the world. Thoughts of the 900 Jews who committed suicide in the first century on a bare hilltop near the Dead Sea rather than be killed by Titus inspire noble feelings. But the self-imposed Jonestown massacre was not noble or even human. It was incredible in that it resulted from the powerful spell one man could exert over others, persuading them to kill themselves and their children. The incident raises some disturbing questions.

One of them is why such a madman could have continued to break the law and remain in favor with prominent lawyers and politicians. Part of it is no doubt explained by the fact that he could deliver so many activists to promote the candidates and causes of the local political machinery. But I could not help thinking of other reasons.

When the tragic news of this affair first broke on the world, I remember one liberal San Francisco clergyman saying that Jones struck him as "a Bible-belt sort of preacher." Some of the gentlemen of the media described him as a "Fundamentalist." It reminded me of the newsmen who had described the assassin Lee Harvey Oswald as a "conservative activist," rather than the collectivist reactionary he actually was.

But the facts show that Jones was on the other end of the pole from Fundamentalists. Reed J. Irvine pointed this out in his syndicated column of November 13, 1978:

> These articles [in the *New York Times*, *The Washington Post* and the *Washington Star*] mentioned the impact of the long sermons or speeches given by Jones. But they said almost nothing about the content of these speeches. There were only occasional hints as to the convictions, the philosophy that moved this man and his fanatical followers.
>
> The *Washington Star* described his congregation as "fundamentalist," and of the three papers, it was the only one that reported that he was a minister of the Disciples of Christ Church, which has about 1.5 million adherents. The *New York Times* contributed the information, obtained from an interview with Mrs. Jim Jones, that when he was 18, Jim Jones' hero was Mao Tse-Tung. Mrs. Jones said that her husband did not believe in religion, but he used it as a substitute "to bring people out of their superstition." She said that his aim was "a Marxist social group," and that was what he was building in Guyana.

Irvine went on to underscore the Marxist philosophy
reflected in Jones's propaganda sheet, *People's Forum.*
Jones's Marxist philosophy was well known to politicians
and newsmen alike, but they chose to ignore it. Irvine said:

> *The* [*Washington*] *Post*, for reasons known only to its
> editors, withheld this information from its readers,
> upholding a practice that has prevailed for at least the last
> 15 years of playing down or ignoring the ideology of persons
> who commit violent crimes when they are on the left . . . .
> Corrupted by its tendency to recognize no enemies on the
> left, the press had for a long time refused to run exposes of
> Jim Jones, even when they had evidence that he was
> confiscating the incomes of his parishioners, staging phoney
> miracles and even resurrections from the dead, and holding
> marathon services featuring the beating of children and
> compulsory public confessions, often of non-existent sins.
> Leo Ryan had tried unsuccessfully to persuade the national
> media to investigate Jim Jones.

We have every right to ask, "Where was the welfare
department when the child beatings were going on?" Why
was there no great cry from the press? Why were local
bureaucrats and elected officials so timid about moving in
on Jones and his Peoples Temple? Was it because he was so
heavily involved in "social" issues, so devoted to statism,
and so involved with the political left? Eventually, of
course, Jones was investigated and indicted for massive
welfare fraud. But still the press was strangely silent.

Neither Reed J. Irvine nor I would accuse the editors of
the *New York Times*, *The Washington Post*, and the
Washington Star of being Communists. But the Communist
Party is only one of the offshoots of the religion of
humanism. The humanist-statist religion is worldwide,
and one does not have to be a Communist to love it or
espouse the tenets of its faith. There are so many people
devoted to this philosophy that it is often only the
traditionalist, the conservative, or, most of all, the Bible-
believing Fundamentalist who is suspected of being
dangerous.

This is something that is too often missed. The average
citizen, devoted to the state as his supreme benefactor and
provider, is as much a devotee of this doctrine as the

committed collectivist. He is just not as much of an activist. And a degree from a school of journalism or a position with some government agency does not change his faith. He remains a statist. This explains why this doctrine has achieved such a hold on government, the press, liberal religion, and public education. These people are not dedicated Communists, committed to "stamping out free enterprise." They are just deluded people who have lost any sense of a supernatural God Who created the world and performs miracles. Their God has, in every real sense of the word, become the state. And they can belong to a "Christian" church and still worship their god.

Men are more guided by their philosophy of life than they are by the facts. Ask the typical school superintendent or teacher if he is a devotee of the religion of "secular humanism," and he will not even know what you are talking about. Most people don't even know such a thing exists. They only know that, in their estimation, the biggest thing in the world is the collective forces of government, as found in the various innumerable agencies that surround them. They are impressed by its bigness. They are in awe of its power. They follow its dictates unquestioningly. They turn over vast areas of their lives to be planned by social workers, legislators, judges, and bureaucrats. They often do not think for themselves. All of these things are indicative of worship in a very real sense.

More importantly, they feel helpless in the face of statism's relentless march into every area of their lives. The day before the news of Jonestown broke, I had read in Dr. Max Rafferty's column that the consensus now is that the emotion of the 70's is not protest, as in the 60's. The emotion of the 70's is despair. Suicide among black teenagers, unknown thirty years ago, is now the leading cause of death for that group. It is also the leading cause of death among white college-age students. Then—as if to underscore the fact dramatically—910 suicides and murders shocked the world.

But the Jonestown tragedy raises another question. Would government have had a legitimate interest in intervening in the sordid affairs of the Peoples Temple? What does the Bible have to say about such things? In our quest for religious freedom are we saying that government has no legitimate interest in any kind of religion? Are we saying that all religious beliefs, no matter how dangerous and heretical, should enjoy immunity from the law? If not, where do we draw the line? And what kind of guidelines are necessary for us to determine which religions are immune from government intervention?

There are no easy answers to this question. Establishment of religion is a powerful thing and easily abused by depraved men. In an advertisement captioned "The Fastest Growing Church in the World," Keith E. L'Hommedieu writes about the "Universal Life Church." It is apparently a church in name only. Its only tenet of belief seems to be a quotation from its founder, Kirby J. Hensley: "The ULC only believes in what is right, and that all people have the right to determine what beliefs are right for them, as long as they do not interfere with the rights of others." Needless to say, their faith can probably have a broader interpretation than that of any church in the world. The "Rev." Hensley's "church" now has a membership in excess of seven million "ordained ministers." According to the advertisement, he started his "church" by mailing out ordinations from his garage for a dollar each. That's pretty cheap. During the Vietnam conflict, Hensley performed mass ordinations on college campuses. The duly ordained ministers then became exempt from the draft.

The IRS acted in 1966, declared the Universal Life Church a phony religion, and impounded its holdings. Hensley filed suit. On March 1, 1974, according to the advertisement, Judge James F. Battin ruled in favor of Hensley. He said in part, "Neither this court or any branch of this government will consider the merits or fallacies of a religion. Nor will the court praise or condemn a religion. Were the court to do so, it would impinge upon the guarantees of the First Amendment."

The popularity of the movement is simple. Any "ordained minister" can find any two other people, including family members, and form a "church." They then enjoy such privileges as exemption of up to fifty percent of their contributions to "the cause"; housing and automobile allowances; and the option of turning their homes into "religious retreats," thereby avoiding property taxes. Commenting on the success of the movement, L'Homme-dieu, who is chairman of the board of the religious group, says:

> Since the church was founded in 1962, it has attracted members who are movie and TV personalities, businessmen, government officials, lawyers, and doctors as well as all types of working people. During the last 15 years the Universal Life Church has blossomed into a full blown grass roots populace movement. Reverend Hensley is ordaining ten thousand ministers a week and predicts that the church will have over 20,000,000 members by the 1980's. In addition, requests for interviews and TV appearances continue to pour in.

Religion is a very popular thing these days and is easy to start. Just find a few blind fanatics and away we go. We hesitated even to quote the above, for fear there are some people reading this book who would join Hensley to get the tax collector off their backs. How far does the government go to combat such rackets without stepping on the legitimate rights of God-fearing people who have a genuine faith in the Word of God?

The degree to which the state can interfere has been dramatized in the "compelling interest" issue which arose in a controversy in the state of North Carolina. The confrontation between public and Christian education in that state had its background in the state's own attempt to avoid efforts to integrate its schools. The so-called "Piersall Plan" was a scheme to bring public education under a system of private schools which would actually be public schools in disguise. Numerous laws were passed in 1956 to place these private schools under state jurisdiction in order to maintain their quality. The plan was abolished by the Supreme Court, but the laws remained on the books.

In 1974, public education lobbyists began to put pressure on legislators to change state regulations in order to eliminate graduates of Christian colleges from state certification. The Rev. Kent Kelly, of Southern Pines, North Carolina, and Dr. Ed Ulrich, a Christian school official, fought this move and won an apparent victory. Then, in 1977, under pressure from the public education lobby, the state mailed a book of minimum standards, 195 pages long, to administrators of private Christian schools. There had been a law calling for these standards since the 1930's, but it had never been enforced. About the same time, the state passed a law requiring certain testing to be administered by Christian schools as well as public schools.

Becoming increasingly aware of what was happening in other states, the leaders in North Carolina Christian schools resisted the requirements. At one time, seventy-three pastors in the state were threatened with imprisonment for their refusal to yield to what they regarded as an unfair and unprecedented attack on separation of church and state. Thousands of parents and children were technically in violation of the truancy laws and the children were subject to removal from their natural homes to foster homes.

These pastors and parents have cause for concern. The following of the "minimum requirements" would virtually eliminate the distinctive Christian character of their schools. The preface of the "blue book" states, "Any real progress in personalizing teaching and learning must of necessity rest upon a program format emphasizing learning outcomes—knowledge, skills, concepts, understandings and attitudes." When unregenerate educators have the power to regulate "understandings and attitudes" of the pupils in schools that teach all curricula in relationship to the Bible, there is ample cause for alarm.

In listing the subjects to be taught, the book requires the teaching of human sex education. I have before me a brochure mailed out to purchasing agents in public schools from the Educational Division of Hallmark Films and Recordings, Inc. I do not know if it is a division of Hallmark Cards. It is advertising the "Human Sexuality Package." A blurb on the front calls it "a must for face-to-face teaching of sex education, especially for slow learners and the mentally handicapped."

The subject matter is described inside the 7" x 9" folder. The teaching program consists of four elements: 10" x 13" teaching cards, 35mm slides, a 90-minute cassette and a 63-page teacher's guide. There is an illustration of one of the teaching cards and transparencies on the folder showing a nude couple engaged in sexual activity. It is outright pornography.

Besides graphic descriptions of male and female sexuality and reproductive organs, the twenty subjects include such topics as "Male Masturbation," "Female Masturbation," "Same-Sex Relationships (Men)," "Same-Sex Relationships (Women)," "Sexual Intercourse," and "Homosexuality." It is said of these materials, "The teaching cards and slides arouse reaction." You had better believe it! One wonders: if that is what they teach the "slow learners and the mentally handicapped," what do they teach the bright kids?

In a further breach of the faith of these religious leaders, the book of minimum standards describes man as an animal and "relates his development as a product of heredity and environment," according to one report.

The Christian educators in North Carolina were first shocked at the minimum standards, then hopping mad. They claimed the action was a violation of their First Amendment rights. But state officials came back with the argument that the state had a "compelling interest" in matters that went beyond reasonable health, fire, and safety standards—matters such as the state's right to furnish a core curriculum for Christian schools.

Bob Dalton, a North Carolina educator, asks some pertinent questions in his article, *Compelling Interest Vs. Separation of Church and State:* "Suppose that the 'proof of education' is insufficient? What then? What courses would the state see as necessary to a 'core curriculum'? Evolution? Sex education? What is 'satisfactory student progress'? Satisfactory by whose standards? Who is a qualified teacher? Who has the right to enforce 'compulsory' education?"

This writer puts his finger on a problem. If the state has a "compelling interest" in church schools, what will the guidelines be? Who will establish the guidelines? Whose philosophy will determine those guidelines? In our case in Tennessee, we were finding it difficult to resist any government control over our churches without resisting all government control, if we were going to be consistent. However, many private schools in North Carolina *agreed* that the state had a compelling interest in these matters, and the private school community became divided in its relationship with the state.

The Constitution of North Carolina, Article 1, Section 13, says, "All persons have a natural and inalienable right to worship Almighty God according to the desires of their own consciences, and no human authority shall, in any case whatever control or interfere with the rights of conscience."

But that was before the days of public education. If the state officials in North Carolina are ignoring that in the case of church schools, it may be because they are under pressure from the teachers' unions. Indeed, these unions have exerted powerful pressure upon politicians lately. They carry a lot of numerical and financial clout. The upset victory of Senator Jim Sasser over incumbent Bill Brock in Tennessee in 1976 can be attributed in large measure to the fact that Sasser had the support of the educational establishment. The National Education Association and its state organizations can no longer be regarded as mere professional organizations, promoting the causes of good education. The more they organize and coerce, the lower our standard of public education drops. The brilliant constitutional lawyer, William B. Ball, says in his booklet *Litigation in Education: In Defense of Freedom*:

> We have three vast areas of enterprise now in the United States, each of which operates on the principle of "expand or die." One is business, another is unionism, and the third is government. Under this view, the reason for government is government.

Now, the lava has not quite set hard in the area of

education. But can we see what is in the making? At worst, it is a *criminally enforced* institutionalizing of every child in the public educational system, which will be the domain of unions, whose interests may run counter to those of the child, his parents, and the taxpayers. The citizenry will be forced, under criminal sanction, to support government schooling at financial levels set by the unions. The values inculcated in these schools will be dictated by elites who intend to mold a secular humanist society.

One problem their organizations face is that while teachers' unions are negotiating fat new contracts under the guise of "quality education," the taxpayers are asking, "Where is the quality you have been promising? Why do test scores continue to go down?" In the Christian schools, children are receiving a far superior education at the hands of dedicated teachers who are working for a fraction of the salaries of public teachers. Declining attendances and job cuts in the public schools also pose a problem for the teachers. No wonder they consider the private Christian schools a threat.

The growing number of illegal teachers' strikes reveals the kind of quality the union moguls are really concerned about. At the beginning of the 1978 school year, teachers in Philadelphia won a new contract calling for the starting salary to go from $10,070 to $11,580. The average salary rose from $19,600 to $22,540. In Boston, teachers had to vote against their union leadership to accept the city's generous offer and go back to work so the city's 70,000 pupils could begin school. Meanwhile, the teachers' union in Alaska won a starting salary of $20,059. That is for nine months' work with two weeks off for Christmas. It ought to buy a lot of "quality."

Pastors and Christian school administrators have every right to be wary of growing interference with their church schools, when the evidence is that the vast public school monolith, with its huge share of public funds and its ranks of jealous teachers, has played a role in instigating the recent attacks. There is special cause for concern when those attacks come so often under the guise of "concern for quality education" which Christian school officials know very well is a phony concern. As one irritated North Carolina pastor, Dr. Bob Settle of the Tabernacle Baptist Church in Hickory, North Carolina, revealed:

If the State is saying, as news reports imply, that the issue is *church rights vs. the right of every child to have an education*, it is immediately obvious that the State is slanderously—insultingly—attacking the integrity of the church! Test results indicate the good job church related private schools are doing in educating our children. Results on Metropolitan Achievement Tests administered to students at Tabernacle Christian School over the past seven years show an achievement of more than one grade level above the national norm.

For centuries it has been the church that has built orphanages all over the world. It is the church that went into Korea in the aftermath of war and built orphanages to take care of ten thousand half-breed orphans, fathered by American soldiers—children left to eat out of garbage cans or die. *It is the church* that raises the strongest voice in America against the murderous slaughter of millions of unborn babies. Where is the power of the State when tens of thousands of babies are slaughtered in our fine hospitals? Who is *genuinely* concerned about the future of children in this State?

If the State says the issue is Church rights vs. the right of the child to have an education, we cannot escape the insulting charge: "The Church has no integrity; the Church is a dangerous threat to children!" We ask the State to be extremely careful in its remarks, and in its actions.

Another pastor, Kent Kelly, retorted, "I don't think the state has a valid concern for these children at all. They are just trying to prove you don't monkey with the state bureaucracy." He went on to say, "I think the state has proved over the last 100 years it is totally incapable of insuring quality education for anybody. They don't have the personnel to see the job is being done. In a . . . little office in Raleigh are two men who are supposed to oversee the quality of education for 55,000 students in nonpublic schools. It's an absurdity."

The question of compelling interest remains to be answered fully. One observation that has come out of my research is that it is not much of a question as long as the "religion" has a statist or socialistic coloring, or as long as it does not interfere with the pet projects of social planners. But there *is* special concern when churches engage in educating their children. That is the one function of religion which stirs more opposition than any other. It is at the heart of all religious freedom considerations. What the Christian schools are saying is that the state is, indeed, establishing and fostering a religion completely contrary to the faith held by Christians everywhere, and that the lifestyle mandated by the Scriptures has been so seriously threatened by the humanist teaching that churches have been forced into the task of educating their own children.

The lifestyle issue might be one of the most noticeable ways to determine the validity of a true religion, if the state has to determine that. It requires only a surface appraisal to see that the drugs, free sex, power-hungry tactics, and Marxist philosophy of the Peoples Temple bore no resemblance to the Christian Scriptures. Nor do the libertarian precepts of the Universal Life Church. The fundamentalist Christian, however, can demonstrate from the Book he holds dear that he is at least making an attempt to live by it. Indeed, that is why so many pastors have added painfully to their already overcrowded schedules in order to begin educating children. They certainly did not need any more work to do.

Pastors across America have not only added immeasurably to their work, but have created huge financial burdens for their churches in order to assume the task of education. Our church has underwritten the Berean Academy ministry at a cost of thousands of dollars per year in addition to all income generated by the school. Thousands of Christian teachers in America have paid the cost of a college education, and then sacrificially accepted teaching jobs in Christian schools at less than half the average salary of their public school counterparts because they actually do "believe in children" and their potential for the future and they see that that potential is being endangered by the humanistic schools. Hundreds of thousands of Christian parents pay their taxes and then pay the additional cost of a private Christian education because it is that important to them. Evidence of a lifestyle that backs up what these people say they believe is not difficult to find, if the state would only take the trouble.

More than anything else, it is the product of these schools the statist enforcers hate. They are generally law-abiding, well-educated, and courteous, and they enter society as leaders. The students in Christian schools have proved that they are educated in a superior system. And they are being trained that way at a tremendous sacrifice of time and energy. The evidence of a committed Christian lifestyle is thrown into focus perhaps more dramatically in the field of Christian education than anywhere else.

Appearing before the IRS hearings on the proposed nondiscriminatory guidelines for private schools in Washington on December 5, 1978, Senator Strom Thurmond of South Carolina pointed out that not only is this true, but these educational institutions are relieving state and federal budgets of huge costs that would otherwise be incurred by taxpayers. He estimated that if the proposed IRS procedures for private schools caused only fifteen percent of these schools to shut their doors, it would cost two billion dollars for the government to assume the task of educating their students. As nowhere else in church-state conflicts, the Christian schools have proved abundantly that they are not threatening the futures of parents and children. The state ought to leave them alone.

While Christian educators were battling it out with the bureaucrats in North Carolina, their brothers in Kentucky scored a significant victory in the courts on the minimum standards issue. Franklin Circuit Judge Henry Meigs ruled that First Amendment considerations far out-weighed any "compelling interest" the state might have in imposing minimum standards on church schools. Ruling in favor of the members of the Kentucky Association of Christian Schools, the judge said, "Quite the contrary, the overwhelming weight of substantial probative evidence conclusively shows the state's efforts to be but poorly conceived, ill-defined and quite direct interference with plaintiff's religious liberty." Judge Meigs said that the two days of testimony in the case "fails to demonstrate more than a scintilla of colorable state interest" in the operation of these church schools.

It does not lie within my domain to draw up guidelines for whether or how government should regulate religious racketeers and phonies. But one thing is sure: The booming Christian education movement in the United States does not fall within the same category as Jonestown or the Universal Life Church. And another thing is equally clear. To diminish and kill religious freedom in the United States would do immeasurably more harm than an army of men like Jim Jones. On the contrary, if the socialist doctrine succeeds in taking over our national life, strangling our churches, another kind of harm will come. Kyung Rai Kim, a Presbyterian layman from Seoul, Korea, told what happened when the churches lost their freedom in North Korea:

> More than 95 percent of the Christians in Northern Korea have escaped to Southern Korea since the Korean War. Before the liberation in 1945, Northern Korea had 1,500 Protestant churches, but there is none there now. There are 116 church buildings remaining, but they are not Christian churches. In 1945 in Southern Korea there were only 1,200 Protestant churches. Today there are 4,200. During the Korean War the Communists killed 1,650 ministers and shot more than 1,600,000 Northern people including 125,000 Christians .... There are no true Christian churches in Northern Korea since the 1945 liberation.... There are churches, but they are Communist-run churches.
>
> In Pyongyang, in 1946, an educational ministry was developed to do away with the Christian churches. The educational minister sent secret police during worship services to hear the ministers preach. The ministers who preached the gospel of Christ were accused of being against the government and were arrested .... Later they were shot. The government made public examples of the ministers by torturing them. An evangelist friend of mine, Lee Chang Whan, was killed .... The Red police stripped him naked, bound him, and put him into an empty water pool. It was 17 degrees below zero that day. They filled the

pool solid. My friend froze to death in 30 minutes. Then the
police exhibited his body to the people....

In January, 1951, 250 pastors were killed by the
Communists on the same day in the same place in Hong Jai
Dong, Seoul, Korea. The Red Police made holes through the
pastors' hands with an ax and bound them hand to hand
with an iron thread, and they shot them. In February, 1951,
at Won Dang Church, Chen Ra Nam Do Province, Red
soldiers burned 83 Christians with gasoline.... We Korean
people in the Korean churches know what communism is.
Many American Christian leaders do not know what
communism really is.

While my readers recoil in horror, they might ask
themselves which is the greater evil—statism or freedom of
religion?

13
HOW BIG IS THE PROBLEM?

When I started this project, I thought I might be able to come up with some estimation of the number of churches that were involved in litigation. I have left off counting. The problem has grown to mammoth proportions. The church-state conflict has become one of the hottest issues of this decade. In 1978, governor's races in Florida and Texas were heavily involved in the church-state controversy. A complete catalogue of the cases in court in the U.S. would be impossible. Here is just a sampling:

In Omaha, Nebraska, the Rev. Everett Sileven has been embroiled in controversy with the state over the operation of Faith Christian School, an educational ministry operated by the church of which he is the pastor. In February, 1978, Superintendent Neal Lancaster of the Cass County School District visited the church school with the sheriff at his side. On March 1, he returned with warrants for the arrest of Sileven and his assistant pastor.

They were charged with "illegal operation of a private school" because they had not sought licensure or accreditation for their church school. This case involved the unexplained substitution of another judge halfway through the case, a tactic believed by some observers to have been intended to remove a judge thought to be open to the church school's pleas.

In Tampa, Florida, a good friend of mine, Scotty Drake, pastor of the Good Shepherd Baptist Church, became involved in litigation with the state over licensure of the Tampa Bay Children's Home, a ministry of his church. The Good Shepherd Baptist Church is fighting efforts to close down the home.

In Tjunga, California, the Rev. Ed White was fighting to keep his church school open after the state fire marshal's office demanded a separate certificate of occupancy for his school ministry. The church, Baptist Church of the Foothills, had already obtained a certificate of occupancy. White was charged with being the owner and operator of an illegal school.

In Hutchinson, Kansas, Evangelist Bill Cowell became the victim of bureaucratic and community harassment when the Hutchinson Police Department sent an undercover agent to infiltrate his home for girls, Victory Village, located on a 117-acre tract on the outskirts of town. When the state pressed for licensure, the home was accused of cruel disciplinary procedures. As usual, the newspapers portrayed the preacher as some kind of weird child-beater. Cowell's girls were taken away while the case was pending in court. Rex Fuller, writing in the *CLA Defender*, pointed out that even a dirty film peddler gets to keep his filthy stuff while his trial is pending, but the evangelist lost his right to keep the girls to whom he had ministered.

In Solon, Ohio, the city is attempting to stop the Rev. Marion Wojnarowski from starting a church in a ranch-style home situated on one and one-half acres of land. They have threatened to lock the doors of this new church facility.

In Concord, New Hampshire, the city tried through

zoning regulations to prevent the operation of the Heritage
Christian School, a ministry of the New Testament Baptist
Church. The church won in the State Supreme Court on
December 9, 1977.

In Harvey, North Dakota, the Rev. and Mrs. Peter Dyck
were charged as criminals for having their four children in
Wells County Christian Academy. The complaint read in
part: "The father, Peter Dyck, has willfully refused to take
his children to the Harvey Public Schools, the school that
the children should attend."

In Seymour, Indiana, the Seymour Baptist Church is
being sued by the Department of Public Welfare for
operating its Kiddie Kollege without a license from the
state.

In Brandon, Florida, the Rev. Robert Gustafson and the
Grace Community Church were denied a permit to
construct a building on ten acres of ground for the purpose
of beginning a Christian school.

Churches and schools in dozens of states are protesting
not only the proposed IRS guidelines for determining
nondiscriminatory practices for private schools but also the
unemployment tax levied against church schools. The
Christian schools in South Carolina, with that state's
Christian Schools Association attorney, Orin Briggs, won a
temporary restraining order prohibiting the state from
levying the taxes until the case is settled. In our case in
Tennessee, Judge Wilson dismissed the case because of
"lack of jurisdiction."

The battle is growing. Admittedly, many of the court
cases are instigated by Christian ministries. Licenses are
being refused, taxation is being resisted, controls are being
ignored that once many of us would not have been much
concerned about. But this position must not be interpreted
as anti-government or anarchist. If anyone believes in a
system of laws and restraint, it is the people who believe the
Bible. Rather, it is a growing awareness of the dangerous
trends inherent in litigation against church ministries. We
believe we are fighting for our very lives. Of one thing we
are sure: that God ordained and established government

does not mean He intended for it to be used against the
people who are attempting to believe and live by the Holy
Scriptures. Although we are willing for our faith to be
tested, we are unwilling to accept the kind of society in
which our children and grandchildren will not enjoy
freedom of worship. And many of our modern heroes of
faith have shown that they are willing to die for that
freedom.

The question is whether there are enough Christians
who are willing to *live* for it. The current church-state
conflict has convinced me that our biggest sin is that of a
lifestyle inconsistent with what we profess to believe. One
of the most dramatic illustrations of the power of a unique
lifestyle emerged from the farmlands of Wisconsin.

The Amish people in America trace their roots back to
the Anabaptists of the sixteenth century who remained
distinct not only from the Roman Catholic Church but from
the emerging Protestant denominations as well. They are
committed to a life of rural simplicity, believing that to
mesh with urban life and progress is to destroy the
distinctive character of their faith. Indeed, this was the
practice of the Anabaptists in Holland, England, and other
Old World countries. The Old Order Amish believe that
their salvation is contingent upon maintaining a church
community that is insulated from the world around them as
far as possible.

An important part of this sect's belief is that they stay
close to the soil, maintaining a strict rural heritage for their
children. Members are required to make their living
through farming and closely allied pursuits. The *Ordnung*
is a book that details the rules of their church and
community life, and gives a clear application of their faith
as they see it taught in the Bible. Upon baptism, Amish
young people, having confessed their faith in Christ,
assume for themselves firm obligations to maintain and
support the Amish way of life. This means, for one thing,
that they will go to work on the farms, learning from their
fathers the way of the land and the way of the Lord.

The Old Order Amish do not object to elementary

education in the public schools, since they say they want their children to be able to cipher and read the Scriptures. However, they feel that public education beyond the eighth grade steers their children away from the closely held rural values that are an integral part of their faith.

High school education emphasizes intellectual attainment, competitiveness, and the world's version of success, but the Amish emphasize "informal learning-through-doing; a life of 'goodness' rather than a life of intellect; wisdom, rather than technical knowledge; community welfare, rather than competition; and separation from, rather than integration with, contemporary worldly society."

The state of Wisconsin took Jonas Yoder and Wallace Miller to court for violating the compulsory attendance laws of the state requiring children to remain in school until age 16. They were convicted in the lower court, charged with criminal truancy, and threatened with jail sentences, but they still clung to their convictional beliefs. The State Supreme Court held that they were entitled to their First Amendment rights and ruled in favor of the respondents, Yoder and Miller. The Court's opinion stated briefly:

1. The State's interest in universal education is not totally free from a balancing process when it impinges on other fundamental rights, such as those specifically protected by the Free Exercise Clause of the First Amendment and the traditional interest of parents with respect to the religious upbringing of their children.
2. Respondents have amply supported their claim that enforcement of the compulsory education requirement after the eighth grade would gravely endanger if not destroy the free exercise of their religious beliefs.
3. Aided by a history of three centuries as an identifiable religious sect and a long history as a successful and self-sufficient segment of American society, the Amish have demonstrated the sincerity of their religious beliefs, the interrelationship of belief with their mode of life, the vital role that belief and daily conduct play in the continuing survival of Old Order

Amish communities, and the hazards presented by the
State's enforcement of a statute generally valid to
others. Beyond this, they have carried the difficult
burden of demonstrating the adequacy of their
alternative mode of continuing informal vocational
education in terms of the overall interests that the
State relies on in support of its program of compulsory
high school education . . . .

4. The State's claim that it is empowered, as *parens
patria*, to extend the benefit of secondary education to
children regardless of the wishes of their parents
cannot be sustained against a free exercise claim of
the nature revealed by this record, for the Amish have
introduced convincing evidence that accommodating
their religious objections by foregoing one or two
additional years of compulsory education will not
impair the physical or mental health of the child, or
result in an inability to be self-supporting or to
discharge the duties and responsibilities of
citizenship, or in any way materially detract from
the welfare of society.

This decision was later upheld by the U.S. Supreme Court,
which stated:

Formal high school education beyond the eighth grade is
contrary to Amish beliefs, not only because it places Amish
children in an environment hostile to Amish beliefs with
increasing emphasis on competition in class work and
sports and with pressure to conform to the styles, manners,
and ways of the peer group, but also because it takes them
away from the community, physically and emotionally,
during the crucial and formative adolescent period of life.
During this period, the children must acquire Amish
attitudes favoring manual work and self-reliance and the
specific skills needed to perform the adult role of an Amish
farmer or housewife. They must learn to enjoy physical
labor. Once a child has learned basic reading, writing, and
elementary mathematics, these traits, skills, and attitudes
admittedly fall within the category of those best learned
through example and "doing" rather than in a classroom.
And, at this time in life, the Amish child must also grow in
his faith and his relationship to the Amish community if he
is to be prepared to accept the heavy obligations imposed by
adult baptism. In short, high school attendance with
teachers who are not of the Amish faith—and may even be
hostile to it—interposes a serious barrier to the integration

of the Amish child into the Amish religious community.

The Amishman's stubborn adherence for more than three centuries to a lifestyle consistent with his professed beliefs speaks eloquently. And this landmark Supreme Court decision is so crucial to the matter at hand that it bears very close examination. The State Supreme Court's decision, later upheld by the U.S. Supreme Court, said first of all that the state's claim to have a "compelling interest" that overrides the First Amendment rights of the parents and children in this case "is not totally free from a balancing process when it impinges on other fundamental rights." In other words, the belief by the educational establishment that they are the only lawful guardians of the future welfare of children in this country was not sustained by the Court. Parents and children still have rights, upheld by the U.S. Constitution, which are not canceled out by the state's compulsory attendance laws. This is extremely important, since it runs counter to one of the basic tenets of the statist philosophy, that the children are wards of the state.

In the second place, the Court recognized the possibility that values which endangered the religious beliefs of the Amish were being taught in the public schools . This is the claim made also by Fundamentalists who have started their own private schools. This puts the issue of public versus private education (in the case of the Amish, their private vocational education) squarely in the arena of a First Amendment consideration.

The third significant finding of the Court is that the Amish really believed what they said they believed. That evidence was supported by three centuries of a life that demonstrated to the world the sincerity of their faith. First, the Court recognized a *consistency*. These people simply did not change. Whatever the world around them did, it had no effect upon their faith. Their faith was not anchored to the changing fashions of the world but to an earnest conviction of their hearts about the unchanging truth of God's Word. Even those who do not agree with them doctrinally are forced to admit the sincerity of their belief.

The Court also saw in them the *practicality* of their beliefs. The state of Wisconsin was arguing, in effect, that the kind of outmoded, old-fashioned life espoused by the Amish simply would not work in this technological age. But the Court looked at the evidence and ruled that they are indeed a "successful and self-sufficient segment of American society." In contrast to the moral bankruptcy and welfarism of society in general, the Amish demonstrated a record of self-reliant and successful living.

The Court also saw in the Amish a *convictional belief*, demonstrated by their lifestyle. In a court of law, it is essential for the claimant to present some evidence. He cannot simply get on the stand and make a claim for himself. In the realm of faith, it is the holy lifestyle that backs up the claim of faith. Although the mainline denominations and many other professing Christians are yielding to the march of a worldly society, the Amish lifestyle gave evidence that they really believed what they said they believed. Although I am not thoroughly familiar with their creed, their position could well have been based on Romans 12:2: "And be not conformed to this world; but be ye transformed by the renewing of your mind, that ye may prove what is that good, and acceptable, and perfect, will of God."

The thrust of modern public education is to get the child to conform to the mores, the fashions, the pressures, and the competitions of the world. The children all dress with the flair of the fashion designer, pick up the fads of popular movies, and sway to the beat of the same music. Powerful forces in education and publishing take these impressionable young minds and twist them to the dreams of the social planners. Children dutifully crown the sports and entertainment heroes of their peers, running on in endless chatter about their comparative physical and behavioral attributes. Pot, pornography, and perversion are first discussed and then experimented with as the children grow older. Teachers, meanwhile, cranked persistently out of colleges and universities with the same socialistic ideas and poor, twisted morals, cannot help passing on to the children the values that motivate them. Thus, raw, secular humanism is both the god and the force of academic life from kindergarten through graduate school. The Amish saw it a long time ago, rejected it, and stood against it. And they won.

The Court also recognized the fact that public education contained built-in *hazards* to the Amish faith. If the state forced their children to go to the secular school, it would abrogate their beliefs and eventually destroy the Amish way of life. Any knowledgeable Christian will have to say that modern public education is not only anti-Amish, but anti-Christian as well. The reason that education is such a forceful religious issue is that the business of feeding information and values into the minds of children can never be a neutral thing. It is always opinionated and philosophical and, therefore, religious.

For years Christian parents have labored under the delusion that they could send their children to the public schools and somehow it would all work out. But their children have come back to them perverted in mind, broken in spirit, and void of faith. Many of the parents I have counseled with have not understood what happened and have searched for some failure to love their children or be a proper example to them. It never occurred to them that, added to their own weaknesses and failures, there was the massive failure of the giant educational system of this country. And its failure has not been one of inadequate funding or facilities. We have enjoyed the educational windfall from the wealth of the greatest nation in the world. The largest single expenditure from government funds is for education. The failure of our educational system has taken place at its very heart—its philosophy. Whatever massive funds may be voted and expended in the future never can and never will change that.

Perhaps the philosophy that guides our educational establishment is the same one that guides our nation as a whole, and educators have to expound it to meet the demands of the population. If that is true, then it is all the more reason for Christians to reject it, because our Bible

clearly commands us to "be not conformed to this world." If
we permit our children to be nurtured in the "faith" of
Dewey and Marx, it will destroy our way of life, just as it
would for the Amish. There is no more compelling reason
for us to fight every effort to restrain us from educating our
own children in the ways of the Book.

Another thing observed by the Court in *Wisconsin* v.
Yoder was that *the Amish were willing to make whatever
financial and other sacrifices were necessary in order to sus-
tain their children's further education.* They paid taxes like
everyone else. Their taxes went to support a system of
public education. But since that system of public education
threatened their way of life, they were willing to go the
extra mile to support their faith. They maintained,
financed, and manned out of their own pockets and
energies an educational program consistent with their
beliefs. The court was impressed with their sacrifice.

Yoder and Miller were represented in this case by
attorney William B. Ball. In his booklet *Litigation in
Education: In Defense of Freedom*, Ball maintains that the
element of sacrifice is an important legal and practical
argument:

> It is well, however, that administrators of funda-
> mentalist Christian schools take a firm stand against public
> funding of their schools and call upon their people to
> *sacrifice* for Christian education. Probably that form of
> witness, which calls for real personal sacrifice, is going to be
> the answer to the financial problem of the private religious
> school. That was always so with the Catholic schools, which
> were built and maintained out of the very substance of poor
> immigrant families and which are maintained today out of
> substantial personal sacrifices.
>
> At the same time, the idea of witness-through-sacrifice
> should take hold for perhaps an additional reason: it will
> spur better-off people to lend more help to their fellows in
> faith. And it will help Christian people to be willing to be a
> "people apart" from the society of the world—even to the
> point of being deliberately *poorer* "people apart" out of their
> resolve to sacrifice for their faith. Christians are indeed
> being gradually forced to choose between an illusory
> "mainstream" America with its cult of material success and
> something quite different indeed—perhaps something
> better.

I cannot help thinking of the many parents who make great personal sacrifices to send their children to a Christian school like Berean Academy, or of my own wife who has driven old cars and lived in substandard houses for years so her children could have the advantage of a Christian education. On the other hand, there is the inescapable conclusion that there are many parents who say they want their children to be taught Christian values but are unwilling to make the necessary sacrifice in order to send them to a school where the Bible is the center of the curriculum.

Greater, more evident sacrifices will be called for in the future as state pressure upon Christian schools increases. Christian parents are going to have to ask themselves if they are willing to make those sacrifices and if they are spiritually prepared for the rigors that will accompany them.

A final observation by the Court in *Wisconsin* v. *Yoder* is that the state claim that public education holds the power to insure success in the future of the child does not hold up in the face of the evidence. In his dissenting opinion in the U.S. Supreme Court, Justice Douglas wrote:

> On this important and vital matter of education, I think the children should be entitled to be heard. While the parents, absent dissent, normally speak for the entire family, the education of the child is a matter on which the child will often have decided views. He may want to be a pianist or an astronaut or an oceanographer. To do this he will have to break from the Amish tradition.
>
> It is the future of the student, not the future of the parents, that is imperiled by today's decision. If a parent keeps his child out of school beyond the grade school, *then the child will be forever barred from entry into the new and amazing world of diversity that we have today* [emphasis added].

William Lear, a man who finished only the eighth grade and went on to invent the condenser that made the car radio set possible, and then to design the eight-track recorder and the Lear Jet, would be surprised to hear that. So would Thomas Edison, who also did not go to high school. So would

Einstein, who flunked elementary math. It is one thing to admit, as any reasonable person would, that our educational system can contain the tools to equip young people for the future. But to suppose, as many in the field of education do today, that public education contains some kind of benevolent and all-powerful magic which to deprive the students of will guarantee failure in life, is patently absurd. If our modern educational system has demonstrated anything, it has demonstrated that it cannot guarantee any kind of success for anybody. That is heresy of modern thought.

While we cannot question the sincerity of the venerable jurist, Mr. Douglas, we think he bases his reasoning on some very wrong premises. First of all, he assumes that children are more capable than their parents of making judgments for them concerning their future. Our faith dictates that parents furnish the guidance, authority, and protection for our children until they reach adulthood. Also contained in Mr. Douglas's opinion is the thought that the state has more responsibility to prepare the children for the future than their parents do.

The majority opinion of the Court ran counter to the opinion of Mr. Douglas and observed that the state had failed to demonstrate that depriving the Amish children of a high school public education would do them irreparable harm, or that denying the state the right to compel them to go to public schools would do irreparable harm to the system.

The *Yoder* case in the Supreme Court was a landmark decision, giving hope to Christian parents everywhere that their children do not have to be the pawns of the educational system of an increasingly collectivistic society. There is danger, however, that future cases may confine it to a very narrow interpretation concerning one small minority only. In his booklet, William Ball wrote, "I quite agree with Gerrit Wormhoudt that *Yoder* may be given a very narrow reading in the future, in an attempt to confine it to an isolated situation regarding an ancient peasant people in our midst."

It remains the task of other Christians to demonstrate by their life and convictions that this is not an isolated case. Are there enough people in this country who can demonstrate a distinctive lifestyle based on true, convictional beliefs to turn the secular tide and demonstrate to the courts of the nation that the Bible really *does* make a difference in people? The future of religious freedom in this country may well depend upon it.

14
WHERE DO WE GO FROM HERE?

I sit here, pecking away on my typewriter, reading thousands of words of comments and court transcripts, and I wonder what kind of picture is emerging from all this. I have some clearer convictions forming in my own heart and know a little bit more about what's going on. But to say that anyone has any pat answers would be to furnish my readers with a simplification that is just not there.

As Christians, we obviously cannot become so zealous in our cause that we become anti-government. That would be a grievous mistake. Government is ordained of God, and He never puts His stamp of approval upon a lawless and disorderly society.

And it cannot be predicted with any kind of certainty how the various court cases now pending will come out. I expect that many of them will drag on for years. How some of the individual cases develop is not essential to the message of this book. We have tried only to share some of the issues as they are illustrated by the continuing controversy. Rather than dealing with a political or religious phenomenon, this book has to do primarily with the personal faith of the people described in its pages and with the person who reads it. All of this is so new, so dramatic, that many Christians, and even those involved in the ministries in question, still do not clearly understand the issues. If we have been able to throw some of those issues more sharply into focus for you, then our time and effort have been worthwhile.

I also hope that some honest people in places of governmental responsibility might come to realize that we have a just and defendable cause. Never would we want to leave the impression that, because certain philosophical errors are running rampant in our society, all school officials, bureaucrats, and elected officials are bad. I personally know many good men in government. I believe that much of what is going on is unknown to them, or at least that they do not understand the issues involved. Maybe some of these good men will read this book and think kindly about what we have said. Others, I am sure, will find many things to argue about in its contents.

There may also be many good, earnest Christians who think that we are half mad, that we just enjoy fighting. Maybe if they can comprehend more clearly what we are fighting for, they will lend prayer and moral support to what we are trying to do. That is at least my hope. It is even conceivable that some who did not previously understand the implications of the religious freedom issue will now take up the fight. And perhaps some Christian parents will now be willing to make sacrifices to give their support to the Christian schools.

Some evidence that there are some honest men looking for answers materialized when the public hearings were held on the proposed nondiscriminatory guidelines for private schools on December 5, 1978. There was an indication that some of the people in the IRS labored under the idea that all these private schools *are* segregationist academies. Some of the testimonies may have convinced them otherwise. Some of them may have learned that schools are being started and maintained at great cost and labor because there are sincere Christians who want their children educated according to the precepts of the Bible.

Two of the speakers at the hearings were from our state association. Dr. Bob Kelley, pastor of the Franklin Road Baptist Church in Murfreesboro, said in his speech:

> The third reason we tenaciously renege against this proposed procedure is that our church considers it an historical tragedy that a government agency can use public funds to suppress, harass, and intimidate our churches into a legal battle which we cannot afford. Every member of this panel full well realizes that church-sponsored schools often operate on a thin financial budget. In most cases, they could not grant an abundance of scholarships, nor could they afford large organized recruitment programs. This is an outlandishly and outrageously oppressive proposal. Please be fair with us, my friends. Your proposal would have far-reaching and even deadly effects upon many wonderful Christian schools that are doing more to change the morals of this country than any other force on this earth. And let me make it known publicly that every active member of the Franklin Road Baptist Church—by church vote—is solidly prepared to lose our tax-exempt status (if pressed to this point and we pray this should never happen), in order to preserve our constitutionally and biblically given right to educate our children according to our basic Bible beliefs.

This type of determined commitment can go a long way in showing government that we live by what we preach. And, in the final analysis, it may be the only thing that can win for us. A conviction is something that will not change, even under pressure.

Charles Walker, the able and articulate executive director of the Tennessee Association of Christian Schools, may have been a bit more restrained than the fiery Dr. Kelley, but he was no less committed. We quote him somewhat at length:

> The issue, though it may appear so, has nothing to do with racial discrimination. The issue, stated simply, is the church and its biblical and constitutional right to operate and maintain its ministries without governmental interference.

The schools in TACS have signed a statement of faith which delineates their strong biblical faith. It is our belief that God has commanded our churches to educate the youth of our church family, and also make their services available to any child desiring to attend. Just as our church doors are open to anyone who wants to hear the Word of God preached, so are our schools open to those who want to receive a Christian education . . . .

The proposed IRS regulations are in violation of the First Amendment to the Constitution of the United States of America. The IRS, by establishing these regulations, is making an attempt to involve itself in the day to day affairs of established religion . . . .

We believe that all truth is God's truth. For us to adopt this principle, *we must relate it to our life in all our deeds.* This is done by integrating each subject area into the Christian frame of reference. The two approaches which we use are (1) the teachers, and (2) the subject areas, i.e., math, science, English, social studies, etc. The teachers are born-again Christians who have accepted Jesus Christ as their personal Saviour and have surrendered their lives to serving God in full-time Christian service. They are active in their respective churches, as well as ardent students of the Bible.

Walker then went on to describe how the various subject areas were built around the Word of God. Many other spokesmen for the Christian school movement were equally forthright in their claim that their schools were not begun to avoid integration but were based on solid convictional beliefs. There were a couple of exceptions which seemed to be Christian schools in name only and whose subject matter and policies revealed that they were motivated politically more than biblically in their approach to education. This at least served to show that there was a difference. The hearings presented the committee with a clear picture of the philosophy of the fundamentalist Christian schools, for the first time for some of them. As this struggle unfolds, perhaps that is one of the purposes it will serve. In government hearings and in courtrooms across the land, Christian school activists are making it evident that there are some people in this country who fear God and are willing to face persecution and hardship, if necessary, to live for Him and rear their children for His glory. They are also demonstrating that they are not selfish in this. They are willing to work and sacrifice so that others, as well, may experience the healing balm of God's Word.

Some of the men I talked to have ventured predictions of what the next five years or so will hold in the struggle to preserve religious freedom in America. Jim Hefley, a fellow author on Signal Mountain, has written an excellent book, *Textbooks On Trial*, on the textbook controversy in which Texas textbook analysts Norma and Mel Gabler are involved. In commenting on what the future holds, he says:

> The National Education Association is the most visible promoter of the goals of progressive education. And it has never denied its program for educator power. The Gablers worry that if the NEA reaches its goals, an academic-political dictatorship could be established over public schools. Private schools will be harassed by bureaucratic rules until they fold or conform.
>
> But the Gablers obviously believe there is hope that this situation can be averted. They believe the failures of progressive education are now so apparent that a grassroots revolt is inevitable. Even the most ardent progressives cannot deny that there is plentiful evidence for concern about American education in a society that seems to be retrogressing academically, morally, and socially.

Part of that grassroots revolt can be seen in the current taxpayer's revolt. Those of us in private education say, "More power to them." If the population at large can reverse the trends in public education without threatening religious freedom, then for the children's sake we are for it. It is not necessarily a free educational system that has imperiled the future of this nation; it is the philosophy of humanism that controls it.

Levi Whisner thinks there definitely will be an acceleration of litigation against churches. Like many of those who have been through the heat of the battle, he believes that the roughest days for religious freedom are ahead of us, and that there will be many who will fall away because of the persecution.

Dr. Roy Thompson, the president of the Christian Schools of Ohio, fears that the church will lose its tax-exempt status in the future. He thinks this will work a hardship on the churches, but will serve to strengthen true believers. He could be right. We wonder how many Christians would give to their churches if they could not claim the exemption.

Charles Walker, Executive Director of the TACS, believes trends will develop in three areas. First, he sees current litigation as the beginning of a definite move by forces within federal and state governments to "entangle church schools with bureaucratic rules and regulations," leading to much more "direct conflict" between fundamentalist church schools and government. He sees the battle being fought fiercely in the next few years, finally deciding the fate of religious freedom under the U.S. Constitution. In view of his projection, I am wondering what this country will be like if we lose. I wonder if it will be the kind of society we want our children and grand-children to grow up in.

Another piercing question Christians are going to ask themselves is if they are willing to stand with those who are fighting to preserve their religious freedom. It is sad that we often have to fight other professing Christians as well as humanistic bureaucrats.

This brings us to Walker's second observation about the future of this struggle. He sees a split developing in the ranks of Christians. Particularly, he anticipates that nominal Christian schools will stand with the forces threatening fundamentalist churches because they will not want the pressure that might be brought to bear upon their own schools and institutions. Even in the fundamentalist ranks, there is the danger that those who are guided more by expediency than conviction will stand against their brothers.

This would work a further hardship on the Funda-mentalists in future litigation, since government will be able to use their testimony to demonstrate that the claimants' position is not necessarily that of the Christian church as a whole. If those involved in the fight can win some hard-earned victories, however, many of their brothers will be quick to reunite with them in order to enjoy the freedom they win.

Walker thinks that many of the leaders in church schools which are based on sound biblical principles will go to jail for their beliefs in the next few years. Those in nominal Christian schools, on the other hand, will readily comply with the increasing regulations in order to keep peace. He says that the IRS hearings revealed that there are two distinct types of "Christian" schools. There is the type that may have been started in reaction to lowering academic performance in public schools, or the integration issue, but which have little emphasis upon biblical principles of God-centered subject matter, separation from the world, and high standards for personnel. The other type that emerged is the school that says all subjects must be taught in the light of the Scriptures. In elaborating on this, Walker said: "What is really going to hurt us is the ostensibly Christian schools started for segregation—'white flight' schools— which are little more than public schools with a Christian name."

This Christian educator is deeply concerned about the number of people in the private school movement who are either ignorant of, or uncommitted to, the dynamic philosophy that is at the heart of a true Christian school. That philosophy, of course, is readily available. It is found in the Bible.

The third trend he sees is a growing effort in schools which are guided by a sound philosophy to integrate all subject matter and activities into the pure teachings of the Scriptures. Our movement is very young, and it takes years to build an adequate curriculum and procedural policy. Having been in the Christian education movement for years, I have no difficulty believing that every subject area can be taught in its proper relationship to the eternal truths reflected in the pages of Scripture. Reading, writing, math, science, and social studies were not invented by some bureaucrat in an HEW office nor by a representative of the NEA. They sprang forth from God's created universe. We are all very excited about developing future curricula to

add to some excellent sources we already have and to har-
monize subject matter with the true teachings of the Bible,
teach character, promote strong family values, and motivate our students to be servants of God.

William Ball sees the struggle continuing along the lines
of four principal areas that have already been contested:

1. Compulsory attendance.
2. State control of private education.
3. Rights of conscience in public education (including
   the problem of value impositions).
4. Denial of distributive justice in the use of tax funds
   (including enforced contribution to programs
   insupportable in conscience).

Ball points out that proponents of public education are
horrified at any suggestion that the compulsory attendance
laws can be abridged, thinking that compulsory
attendance is the one legal principle upon which the public
education system can survive. Opponents, he notes, can find
a sizable weakness in that idea in the fact that the laws are
so different from system to system. In his booklet, quoted
several times earlier, he says, "There is great variety in the
compulsory attendance laws of this country. Each
particular compulsory attendance law is contended to
represent an absolutely unchallengeable expression of
public wisdom. Yet age requirements under these statutes
vary considerably—so that in one state the public wisdom
dictates that a child be formally educated until age
fourteen, while in another it is accepted as fact that he
needs education until he is eighteen."

Ball goes on to say, "Then there is the whole question of
what a child must attend in order to be 'in attendance.'
Some statutes require that the child attend a school, while
others speak merely of his attending a public school or
receiving 'equivalent education'—which latter term does
not even refer to a school. Then again, a question arises as to
when a school is a school or when equivalent education is
equivalent. Who shall say, and according to what
standards? The public wisdom is unclear on these matters."

Ball points out that there is a legitimate question as to whether compulsory attendance laws are constitutional at all. The constitutionality of the law in specific cases has been tried in court, but the general principle has not. Some parents may want to challenge that fact.

In the important area of state control of private education, Ball surmises that many regulations have been made possible by the desire of Americans to be lawful, to use the "standard brand," thinking it to be superior because it has the government's stamp of approval upon it. His experience has shown him that such is not the case: "Much of the regulatory matter—rules, regulations, guidelines, norms, forms—is incredibly poor stuff, embracing leading definitions, internal contradictions, resolute departures from statutory authority, vagueness, all manner of unenforceable precatory language, and, withal, greedy, unconstitutional overreaching in every direction."

He then cites a comical exchange in which he was cross-examining a state official. The dialogue revealed that the regulations were too vague to be binding, that they were unenforceable, and that the official did not even understand them himself. In every organization there are the seeds of its own destruction or survival, and Ball believes the inadequate, poorly defined bureaucratic regulations themselves make the state's position in education very vulnerable. His comments on this are most encouraging and revealing:

> I believe the educational monopolists, with that large mass of patently unconstitutional regulation, have given us the very instruments we need to make breakthroughs for educational freedom. To assure that these are utilized in the struggle for freedom, however, we need perceptiveness and an aggressive spirit of challenge. I salute Pastor Whisner and his associates on both counts. I believe they could have made, in the long run, some sort of financial peace with the state. They could have agreed to go along, and the state would have been willing to temporize, undoubtedly, in leading them through the endless maze of the chartering process. Pastor Whisner refused to make a corrupt bargain. Without understanding all of the legal ramifications of the 600 "minimum standards" of the State Board of Education,

he was perceptive enough to realize that these impinged upon the religious, educational, parental, and economic liberties of his people. He did not, therefore, quail at being presented with the state's "standard brand" of regulation. He did not knuckle under, sighing, "Well, it's the law." And so he successfully resisted.

Ball says that if in the next few years we take the initiative to challenge some of these poorly defined regulations in the courts, we can win some victories.

He feels that the rights of conscience in public education have not been litigated well enough or extensively enough. One of the most seriously challenged issues is parental rights. Ball laments that our welfarism has produced an irresponsibility that leaves many parents wanting someone else to take the burden off them. There are many others who do not care. But Ball thinks the parents who feel their values are threatened by the statist philosophy can win in court.

Another area is the use of public funds to promote secular humanism, now defined by the Supreme Court as a religion. The burden of proof would lie heavily upon the challengers, but he thinks it can be done. If the constitutionality of the establishment of this religious idea through the use of public money could be successfully challenged in court, secular humanism would become illegal in public schools, just as the Bible and prayer are now.

Furthermore, Ball believes these values can be challenged on an individual basis. In *Engel* v. *Vitals* a twenty-two word prayer was found to be unconstitutional. This is the famous case that "threw the Bible out of the public schools." Ball observes:

> Look again at Engel. The prayer was the merest expression of theistic sentiment, which, even if persisted in, was not going to radically alter any child's life. Yet that twenty-two word prayer is now unconstitutional. Compare that with such programs as MACOS or HEW's latest job, "The New Model Me." These latter programs go to the very vitals of a child's existence, probe into his family relationships, directly attack Christian values pertaining to many areas of morality, and are capable of severely disorienting a child

psychologically .... Can we venture to say that a handful of
people who didn't like Bible reading and praying have
rights superior to other people who do not want their
children's moral structure destroyed?

In the remaining area of the struggle, distribution of
public funds, Ball believes that for parents to have to pay
for a private education because public education has failed,
and still support the failing public education system with
their taxes, is double payment and is wrong. And he
believes it can be successfully challenged:

> To what extent should citizens be forced to contribute to
> maintaining a system of education that, in conscience, they
> must decline to support? Public education is widely
> becoming low quality education. The extravagance of its
> aims, its yielding to powerful pressure groups in terms of
> spending, and its politicization are rendering it the most
> extravagant of all enterprises in this country. Its supporters
> constantly play up the problem with which they say it must
> grapple and point to public schools as victimized by
> ungrateful legislatures and an uncomprehending public.
> On the contrary, it is gorged with public funds. In states
> such as Pennsylvania public schools absorb fifty percent of
> the entire state budget. Ours is the most expensive schooling
> the world has ever known, and its incompetence is rapidly
> becoming worse. Many people therefore may feel that on
> purely secular grounds, they ought not to be required to
> contribute to the support of bad education ....
>
> We must get ourselves better in hand: we are not yet
> slaves of a People's Republic. We ought not cringe in hopes
> of keeping a residue of freedom. We have a great measure of
> freedom: let us utilize that boldly in order to get whatever
> proper freedoms we now lack.

What Ball is saying bears close attention. We do not have
to throw up our hands and surrender to the supposed
juggernaut of socialism. We need, rather, to take the
offensive and win freedom for ourselves and those
generations that the Lord may choose to permit to follow us.
And he is saying that innumerable agencies and
bureaucracies are not invincible, unchangeable
depositories of public wisdom. The ideas that most threaten
us are the most weak and vulnerable. And we still have a
great measure of freedom and opportunity in which to win.
But if we will not be stirred by the issues and use our

freedom to maintain our freedom, we will lose religious freedom in this country.

What lies ahead probably depends more on some of the readers of this book than it does on the array of lawyers, dedicated ministers, and determined parents who have been portrayed here.

15

JUDGE THRASHER AND 300 OTHER PEOPLE

March 23, 1979, started out like many other days in Chattanooga—rainy. A strategy meeting at 6:30 in the morning had brought a number of preachers, the officers of the TACS, our two local attorneys, and the law team from the Christian Law Association to the Downtowner Inn for breakfast.

We had obtained a temporary restraining order from Chancellor Wilkes T. Thrasher against the collection of the unemployment tax. The state was challenging that order on the grounds that the state anti-injunction provision did not permit it and that Judge Thrasher's court had no jurisdiction in the case.

For more than two hours we were drilled in what the issues required of us. I was one of five pastors who might be expected to testify in the case. Our strategy was to introduce as much testimony as possible in this hearing in order to provide a good basis upon which to build our case in future hearings, thus the relatively large number of witnesses.

For drama, the court hearing rivaled anything ever seen on television. Judge Thrasher had been undergoing treatment for cancer in Houston and had flown back to Chattanooga to hear this case. All of our churches had been praying for his recovery. David Gibbs of CLA had undergone gall bladder surgery only three weeks before and was still weak and in pain. Our first choice for witness, Dr. Charles Britt, a pastor in Memphis, had been in an all-night prayer meeting a week earlier with members of his church.

By the time Judge Thrasher gaveled the case open, 300 people had arrived for the hearing, far more than the 100 seats could accommodate. They were standing in every available inch of space, sitting on the floor, and spilling out into the rotunda. Judge Thrasher, after courteously addressing the crowd, called the attorneys into his chambers. One of the things he said disturbed our counsel. He said something to the effect that he had previously tried a similar case and ruled against those who were on our side of the question. Our Christian lawyers prayed harder.

Our attorney, David Gibbs, put Dr. Charles Britt, a pastor in Memphis, on the stand. A part of his testimony was later summed up in Judge Thrasher's opinion:

> Reverend Charles Britt testified that his church ... used a Christian curriculum specifically prepared for their school, and that the Christian curriculum is a basic tool which is used by the teachers in teaching the Bible .... He testified that ... his conviction was that it was a sin to have the children not receive a Christian education. In fact, he says that it's a belief that Christian education is indicated and directed by the Lord himself. He says he preaches this concept from the pulpit.

Dr. Britt's testimony was the logical outgrowth of his convictions, that all education is inherently religious and that it is a sin to teach a false religion. This is the essence of what we have been saying. The idea hit the court, the newspapers, and the people of the community like a bombshell.

At one point the dialogue was especially intense, and the silence from the spectators could be felt:

Gibbs: Reverend Britt, if we exhaust our legal means of relief, and the state still seeks to compel you to pay this tax, would you pay it?

Britt: No sir, I could not pay it.

Gibbs: Why could you not pay it?

Britt: It would put me in a position in which I would have to deny my faith, to sin against the Lord, and I could not do that.

Gibbs: Are you aware of the possible consequences of not paying the tax?

Britt: Yes, sir, I have thought about that. I have preached in jails and visited jails often. I have always seen the jails from outside the cell. And I never dreamed that, as a minister, the government would put me in a position where I would either have to sin or go to jail.

Judge Thrasher, two attorneys for the state, and the 300 other people present hung upon every word as Pastor Britt continued: "I certainly do not relish the thought of going to jail. But I would rather go to jail than sin."

When Dr. Britt finished his testimony, the judge turned to me and the other witnesses who had already been sworn. "Nod your heads if you agree that your testimony would be substantially the same," he instructed. We nodded our heads.

After reviewing the arguments of both sides, along with Britt's testimony, Judge Thrasher said, "Reverend Britt said that we have a conviction that our school is headed by the Lord Jesus Christ and that He is the head of the Church. He felt that the Church should, therefore, not be regulated by the State, or ... by the Federal Government as well because he felt that the power to tax was a power to regulate and control the Church and the Church school and that this violated the very basis of his convictional belief."

Then the judge did a little Bible quoting himself, pointing to the example of Daniel and the three Hebrew children. After reviewing again the respective positions of the two sides, he rendered his opinion:

> Now, the Court is of the opinion that Reverend Charles Britt
> was heading in the right direction when he said that the
> Church is to be—is headed by Jesus Christ and that to allow
> a tax or the State to impose a tax would, in essence, be
> regulating the Church and controlling the Church.
> Therefore, it would not be under the head of Jesus Christ,
> but under the head of the State. The Court takes it a step
> further. The Court embraces the words of Thomas
> Jefferson. Thomas Jefferson said, "The best government is
> the government which governs least.". . . The Court is of the
> firm opinion by way of dictum that we've got too much
> United States Government in our lives now and in every
> facet of society. Every time we turn around, there's a new
> rule, a new regulation, a new edict. It's also stated that when
> the Federal Government began to help public schools, they
> wouldn't control it. They wouldn't try to dictate as to the
> policy. We all know the first thing they stopped was prayer
> in the schools. Now they're trying to do away effectively
> with Bible in the schools. This Court feels that the State of
> Tennessee is now about to invade a field that it has no
> business invading. Therefore, the Court, number one:
> respectfully denies the State's position to compel
> compliance with the subpoena; number two: the Court holds
> that it does have jurisdiction over this case; number three:
> the court for the reasons just recited hereby enjoins the
> State of Tennessee from proceeding further with taxation of
> these Church schools.

When a spontaneous round of applause broke out in the
courtroom, the venerable jurist responded with these
words, recorded in the official opinion, "Hold it—there will
be no outburst in this Courtroom. This is a Court of Law."

By the time the crowd thinned out, I found my wife,
Joan, sitting on a bench in the rotunda. The stained glass in
the dome of the old courthouse gave the color of the rainbow
to her tears.

Outside, it had stopped raining. The sun hung over the
hills of Tennessee, and the retreating clouds threw Lookout
Mountain into sharp contrast.

Many battles in the war lay ahead. But this round had
been won. Late that afternoon, I sat in my study
contemplating the events of the day and the things that
were yet to be done. In a few minutes we would leave for a

Christian school rally in Murfreesboro. We anticipated returning home about 3 a.m. At 8 a.m., there was a church board meeting. It had already been a long day.

My phone lit up. It was Judge Thrasher returning my call requesting copies of his opinion.

"Thank you so much for your fine opinion, Judge Thrasher," I said from a depth of appreciation.

"You folks pray for me. The Lord has already given me some victory in this illness," he said.

"We have been, your honor. And we will continue to do so," I said with conviction.

I placed the phone back in the cradle and headed home to take a quick shower. There wasn't much time.

16
WHAT'S IN IT FOR ME?

"Let us hear the conclusion of the whole matter: Fear God, and keep his commandments: for this is the whole duty of man" (Ecclesiastes 12:13).

Some Bible expositors tell us that this is the preacher's legalistic appraisal, and merely the best thing possible for man "under the sun." I am not so sure. I am convinced that nothing can offer as much promise, as much joy, as much happiness and peace, as fearing God and keeping His commandments. I am quite sure that all the turmoil, the confusion, and the conflict on this planet can be traced to a human rebellion against the authority of a benevolent and loving God who wants the best for His creatures. I know that His commandments are not engineered to place an intolerable burden upon men to please the insatiable vanity of an unreasonable deity, but that God in His wisdom created man and knows and desires what is best for him.

That is true not only for the natural man, "under the

sun," but for the regenerate man as well. For those of us who know Him, who delight in Him, who enjoy the brightness of "walking in the light" with an ever delightful and loving Saviour, what could possibly be better than monitoring every decision and every action in the light of what would please Him?

In simple layman's language, I think we "fumble the ball" when we take matters into our own hands. That's what we have done. In many areas of our lives we have ignored conscience, godliness, and conviction, and taken the path of least resistance.

Take me, for instance. I have a nice home in Florida, the only thing left from a business I left twenty years ago to enter the ministry. I long for the day that I can soak up the sun, putter around the house, and rest. I have been taking pictures of scenery and old barns and old churches all over the world. I would like nothing better than to set up an easel, dab a chiseled fitch brush into a glob of acrylic paint, and tell myself I have earned the rest and that after all, the world needs to find an expression of Christianity in the paintings of a retired preacher.

Let the politicians run the world; I'm tired. Let the teachers' unions and the bureaucrats shape the progress of education in this country for the next twenty years. By then I'll be dead and won't know the difference. If Levi Whisner and Roy Thompson and David Gibbs want to make fools of themselves, running around the country like a bunch of redneck zealots, stirring up trouble, let them. That's their business. Ohio's a long way from here.

After all, if the collectivistic society takes over our churches, regulating them to death, it will probably take a while before it hurts *really* badly, and by that time, I'll be retired. Let this young generation of preachers coming along worry about that. I've fought *my* battles. Besides, I have my security to think of. If I make too much noise, the government might cancel my social security or audit my income tax return every year.

And then there is my congregation. Surely, I can't embarrass them by getting involved in an unpleasant and unpopular cause. These are not rabble-rousers. They are nice, middle-class people who work hard and pay their taxes. If we get caught in a squeeze on this thing, we could lose some members and that might hurt us financially.

And besides, I'm busy trying to reach people with the gospel and build my Sunday school. Every Saturday morning I go out with my bus workers to visit the kids on my route. Do you know how hard it is to go from reading a brilliant dissertation by William B. Ball to striking up a conversation with a raggedy, freckle-faced kid who is flunking the fourth grade? I think we can leave the big decisions to other people if we just get out the gospel, don't you? If these parents get to thinking I am some kind of nut, they might not let their kids ride my bus. And that would be bad.

Oh, sure! All of those things have run through my mind, and more that I'm ashamed to admit. The only thing is, when I pick up my Bible, I read over and over again that I am supposed to do what is right: "Therefore to him that knoweth to do good, and doeth it not, to him it is sin" (James 4:17).

That verse makes me awfully lonely. Because I know that no matter what Lester Roloff or Jonas Yoder or anybody else stands for or fights for, even if I get to enjoy the victory they win, God is not going to say to me, "Well done, thou good and faithful servant, for what Lester Roloff did for you!" The important thing is what I have thought, what I have said, what I have done. In the final analysis, in matters of conscience and faith, I am alone with God. And I could not feel at peace painting old Tennessee barns and fishing for snook if I had failed to stand for Him, shunned His righteous cause, and deserted His people who are standing for Him. Nor could I while away my days on a Florida beach when my granddaughter, Meg Metts, has to sit in a classroom and listen to the mad ravings of Dewey and Skinner, or when some young preacher is trying desperately and bravely to preach the gospel of Christ while bureaucrats lurk in every doorway of his church, strangling his ministry. That is neither happiness nor peace. It is stagnation.

And yet, that is the world's picture of success that most of us have fallen for. We think that is happiness. I will just "do my own thing and let the rest of the world go by." That is what has brought the mess on us now. Several generations of Christian parents have ignored the command of God to teach and train their children, shrugging off that responsibility to "professional" educators, and now the chickens have come home to roost. All the while, God was pointing the finger at every father and saying, "That's *your* responsibility!" Now that most fathers have failed, many of them have thrown up their hands in despair and said, "Let the HEW do it." Now, God will surely judge the HEW. But He will also judge every father who has shrunk from his God-given responsibility.

Several generations of church members have been only too willing to let the "professional" ministers handle their religion for them. They have said, "You take care of the sacred part, and we'll handle the secular stuff." And then, when those preachers have fallen under the pressure, or yielded to the temptations and weaknesses common to all men, more and more church members have sighed and said, "The church has failed as an effective entity to cope with the problems of mainstream America." *Baloney.* If the church has failed, it is because most of its members have said, "Let George do it." God will judge worldly churches and apostate denominations, to be sure. But God will also judge every member of those groups on an individual basis.

For decades now, many Christians have gone to the polls, if they even bothered to go at all, with the questions, "Which candidate will help *my* labor union the most?" or "How does this issue affect *my* job?" Then, when corruption rips through Washington, and the welfare rolls bulge, and the bureaucrats add thousands of dollars to their already fat payrolls, they throw up their hands and say, "You just can't trust politicians!" Sorry about that, Bud. They are only as selfish as you were when you voted for what was in it for you rather than for what was right.

For years, many Christians have been joining the

church that has "the best youth program for my children,"
regardless of the fact that the church supports apostasy,
has a worldly standard, and doesn't stand for anything. Our
newspaper church pages look the same as the theater
pages. Larry Jackson, pastor of the Lovelaceville,
Kentucky, Baptist Church, has some succinct comments
about the state of our modern churches:

> Since the average churchgoer is living in pretense and
> has no appetite for real religion it has been necessary to
> make some adjustments. Instead of dedicated worship and
> sacrificial service we have what might be called
> ecclesiastical entertainment.
>
> Today's sophisticated churchgoer can shop through the
> religious page of his Friday paper and find out what will be
> playing in the various churches on Sunday. It will be noticed
> that sometimes it is difficult to distinguish between the
> religious page and the amusement page.
>
> On the religious page it can be noted what Gospel
> celebrities are in town and when they are appearing. A
> church is very fortunate to have a guest appearance by a
> Gospel celebrity. These celebrities usually appear in
> exchange for the privilege of plugging their latest records,
> books, or religious trinkets.
>
> Broken down entertainers who couldn't make it in show
> business have found that by giving their act a religious
> veneer they have a ready market in the churches. Every-
> thing from magicians to broncobusters are [sic] on the
> church circuit .... Family singing groups are particularly
> popular. Most of these groups have successfully modernized
> the old time religion. They keep up with the latest trends,
> styles, and fashions of the entertainment world and add just
> enough religious flavor to get by. These groups have the
> same hair styles, dress, music, and manners of any other
> rock and roll group but they know how to sprinkle their
> songs with choice, standard, religious phrases.
>
> Today's successful religious service has become a
> carefully produced theatrical production designed for the
> delight of the church audience. This entertainment might
> range from operatic arias to country and western hoedowns,
> from Shakespeare to cheap vaudeville acts, but enter-
> tainment [it] is ... nothing more. Audience participation
> shows are also popular. Fun and games for everyone. Prizes
> galore and everyone has a chance to win. Everybody sing.
> It's not raining on the inside. Game shows come in for a big

play. Contests are always big. Participation and competition are tried and proven winners.

The Sunday morning floorshow will regularly feature the same basic format ... a good musical program, guest celebrities, a stand-up comic, and a good master of ceremonies who must also excel in extracting money. A news commentator with religious overtones is always good. All this must run smoothly and fit neatly into the allotted time.

This association of religious truth with mere entertainment has so cheapened the truth that no one takes it any more seriously than they do the patter of a nightclub comic.

If what we want is entertainment let's be honest enough to call it that and quit trying to disguise it as religion.

If this is what we want in our churches, then we almost deserve what we get in America. I know that after men and women have been fighting in the "world out there" all week they want a "religious lift" when they get to church on Sunday morning. Nobody wants to be depressed even more. And there *is* a need for us preachers to dwell occasionally on the lofty, soaring, hope-inspiring promises of God and not spend all our time talking about the problems. But this idea of going to church to get a "religious break," like a coffee break, is at the heart of one of our pet heresies. The truth is, if we would look at the world as God's rightful domain, if we would crown Him King of the "world out there," going forth to conquer rather than being conquered, we would not view the world so much like a bad-tasting secular sandwich between the bread of heaven on Sundays. Did not He say, "These things I have spoken unto you, that in me ye might have peace. In the world ye shall have tribulation: but be of good cheer; I have overcome the world" (John 16:33)?

The early Christians went to the stake with a song on their lips, and not because they had easy circumstances. They sang because they had an unshakable faith that Jesus Christ was Lord, that He had overcome, and that they were the victors. Peace is not a product of easy circumstances and retirement in the sun. It is a product of faith in the mighty, conquering Son of God!

We are going to need in the next few years here in America something of what those early Christians had. And what we will get for ourselves if we take a stand and do what is right is not misery and defeat, but victory in our souls, a song on our lips, and joy in our lives.

What's in it for me? A clear conscience. A bold heart. A victorious life. The joy of serving. Purpose. Fruit. Fulfillment. The protection of the angels. The power of the Holy Spirit that comes through simple obedience instead of cowardly rebellion. Souls won. Children who respect me for standing for my convictions. Future generations who might benefit because I was willing to do right. The chance to live with myself in peace. An opportunity to turn the tide. Crowns of victory. A "well done" from the lips of Him Who is altogether lovely, and for Whom I decided a long time ago I would sell the world if necessary for that one pearl of great price. Try getting *those* with your Master Charge!

Our problem is that we have sold a colossal birthright for a mess of the world's pitiful pottage, and now we are paying for it. And the next few years may decide how great a price it is. True, the Lord may come before then; but that blessed hope should be a purifying factor in our lives, not an excuse for self-seeking negligence.

It all originates in *personal* responsibility. The other day we got a communique from a local school official concerning another of those growing numbers of regulations for church ministries. The secretary gave it to our administrator, John Innes. He read it and put it on my desk with a note, "What do we do about this?" When I read it, I mumbled under my breath, "Why doesn't *he* do something about it? Why do *I* get stuck with all these decisions?" I wanted to call him, but I knew it was no use. Making that kind of decision is, unfortunately, part of my job. There were some questions in my mind as to whether it breached First Amendment considerations. I wanted to call Charles Walker, but I knew he couldn't make the decision for me. Neither could our lawyer. I thought and I thought. I looked around that small office, but there wasn't anybody else there. The buck had stopped.

But I had forgotten about Someone. I wasn't alone. At no time in my life when I make a decision am I alone. I have a personal, living Saviour. He is looking on, and no matter how hard I try, I can't get rid of my responsibility to Him by getting somebody else to make my decisions for me. I have to have my own convictions—my own personal set. God is not going to let me get off the hook by letting someone else live my life for me. And Jesus is wanting to live His life through me.

I can't turn over my God-given responsibility to rear my children to a group of educators down at the little brick schoolhouse, because He is not going to judge *them* for that. He gave that responsibility to me. If God has given me the freedom to vote, and I let the special interest groups and the worldlings do all the voting, guess who is to blame when things go wrong in government? And if I take God's money and divide it among the three major department stores, guess who is to blame if the church fails in its task? And regardless of how much the preacher fails to do *his* job, if I don't witness to my neighbor, guess who shares the blame if he goes to hell?

Jonas Yoder stood against the whole system, just one man. And he won. It got awfully lonely for Levi Whisner on that witness stand that day. Really, it was the faith of one man on trial. Because, although he had some of his constituency standing with him, it was *his personal* convictions that were on trial. Lester Roloff has thousands of friends and millions of radio listeners, but when it got down to cases, none of them could go to jail for him. He had to do that himself.

You can fuss and holler and blame the Communists and politicians all you want to. But this book is not addressed to them. It is addressed to you. I don't have to tell Whisner and Roloff these things; they have already settled them. They can win their victories, but only *you* can win yours.

If you were placed on the witness stand right now and examined for your faith, what would be the outcome? What *do* you believe? I can hear some dear person saying, "I believe what the Baptists believe." Even some preachers, before they got on the stand, have asked their lawyers, "What *do* we believe about this?" But the lawyer is not on trial; the preacher is.

It is past time that we can get by on secondhand convictions, entertainment religion, and letting George do it. You may think that you are not on trial. But you *are*. God is under no obligation to save America or guarantee religious freedom to us. He does not love us any more than He did the Christians in Russia and China. And if we do not *want* biblical Christianity badly enough to live by our convictions and stand for what is right, He is not going to give us something we don't want.

If your lifestyle were to be examined on a witness stand today, how many compromises would be discovered? Your dress? Places you frequent? Business practices? Reading habits?

An interesting and curious thing did turn up in *Wisconsin* v. *Yoder* in the examination of the Amish community: "He also notes an unfortunate Amish 'preoccupation with filthy stories,' as well as significant 'rowdyism and stress.' These are not traits peculiar to the Amish, of course." Of course they are not. But the fact that these things could be found was used against them. They were probably not characteristic in the life of Yoder. But the fact that they could be found in the lives of his brothers was used against him. And they weakened the powerful testimony that this case had.

God gave us freedom. What did He give it to us for? So that we might have better entertainment? So that we might be comfortable in our old age? So that we might have more time to watch television?

He gave us freedom of worship. Why? That we might enjoy a "religious break" for an hour every Sunday morning? Is that what it is all about? Freedom for our gospel quartets to travel from church to church to entertain us? Freedom to go camping on Sunday when we choose to, and then come back to our comfortable churches and sing, "Brethren, We Are Met to Worship"? Freedom to let the preachers and missionaries do our witnessing for us?

Freedom for us to spend most of our time watching football games, buying new appliances and clothes, and talking to our houseplants? I hardly think that's what the pilgrims had in mind.

Somehow, we are going to have to start living by our convictions and facing the problems with an overcoming faith. And somehow we are going to have to let it start with *me*, rather than with all of those other people "out there."

The collectivists have sold us a bill of goods. They have told us that society is a melting pot of all races and creeds and that truth is whatever the consensus of the collective group is at any given time on any given issue. It is one of the biggest lies that has ever been told. God does not wait to see what the group is going to do before He decides what is true. Our Christian faith is not a cafeteria line where we choose whatever everybody else is getting. Nor does it wear the label of the world's "standard brand." Nor is it a new model tailored specifically for this year. Rather than trying to remodel our old-fashioned faith to fit this mad day, we are going to have to alter our lives to fit God's unchanging truth.

In the very zenith of his power as a preacher, the venerable Charles Haddon Spurgeon had to withdraw from the Baptist Union of England. Christendom looked on as his own brothers held a disgraceful meeting and censured him. It hastened his death, but looking around at those who were falling into expediency, worldliness, apostasy, and unbelief he had said, "I will do right if the stars fall out of their sockets!" It may have been one of the secrets of his great power.

If studying these matters of faith, as illustrated in these court cases, has taught me anything, it has shown me that in the final analysis I am alone with God when it comes to my personal convictions and the actions I take based on those convictions. I don't know what the future may reveal in these matters. But whatever it is, I must be prepared to meet it with the courage of my own convictions.

I ask again, my friend, how are you going to vote? What are you going to do? What sacrifices are you willing to make? How are you going to stand?

In the final analysis, you, too, are alone with God and your personal convictions. "And I sought for a man among them, that should make up the hedge, and stand in the gap before me for the land, that I should not destroy it: but I found none" (Ezekiel 22:30).Will that be true in the United States?